AN AMERICAN VOTER

AN AMERICAN VOTER

MY LOVE AFFAIR WITH PRESIDENTIAL POLITICS

JOAN SULLIVAN

BLOOMSBURY

Published by Bloomsbury, New York and London
Distributed to the trade by Holtzbrinck Publishers

Cataloging-in-Publication Data is available from Library of Congress

ISBN 1-58234-201-6

First U.S. Edition 2002

10 9 8 7 6 5 4 3 2 1

Typeset by Hewer Text Ltd, Edinburgh
Printed and bound in the United States of America
by R.R. Donnelley & Sons, Harrisonburg

For My Father

Acknowledgments

A great many books guided me, but the ones to which I am most indebted are Henry Adams's *The Education of Henry Adams*, Paul F. Boller's *Presidential Campaigns*, Timothy Crouse's *The Boys on the Bus*, David Halberstam's *The Powers That Be*, Richard Hofstadter's *The American Political Tradition*, Joe McGinniss's *The Selling of The President 1968*, George Stephanopoulos's *All Too Human*, Hunter S. Thompson's *Fear and Loathing: On the Campaign Trail '72*, Theodore's White's *The Making of the American President 1964* and *The Making of the American President 1968*, Jackson S. Jackson III and William Crotty's *The Politics of Presidential Selection*, and *The Almanac of American Politics 2000*. Enormous thanks also goes to James Dao and his colleagues at *The New York Times* and to David Yepson of the *Des Moines Register*, whose articles I read and reread. For time and advice, I am further indebted to my friends and co-workers from the Bradley campaign and to Christopher Boerboom, Lara Carrigan, David Forrer, and William Georgantas. Finally, very special tribute goes to Karen Rinaldi and Kim Witherspoon, who made this possible, to Flo, who was loving, patient and wise, and to my family, Sullivan, Brown and McPhee, more particularly to my mother, whom I revere, to my sister Martha, who sustained me with her encouragement and to my sister Jenny, who was my greatest resource.

1

No Expectation of Return

Where or when hope fades in a man is as difficult to make precise in date as when hope is born.
—Theodore White, *The Making of the President, 1964*

I T I S A cool dark afternoon in late February, and I am in my fifth month on the Bradley campaign. I have spent the day at the center of UCLA's campus, planning a rally and attempting fitfully to make my cellular phone function properly. I dial again and again, pressing the number buttons harder and harder, and on occasion I get through, but the reception in this plaza is terrible and the tall winter wind has me shivering. It is suprising to feel cold in Los Angeles.

When the time comes for our conference call, I climb to the second floor of Ackerman Union and find a rooftop balcony. Were it not for my extraordinary interest in the outcome, I would skip the call entirely. As it is, I feel like a child rushing toward a radio for the next installment of *The Shadow*. "Who knows what evil lurks in the hearts of men? The Shadow knows." I am twenty-six, a great deal too young to have been a fan of forties radio, but the show's introductory lines, recited to me by my mother, sound oddly

1

wonderful and correct as they emerge from my lips. For a second, no more than a nostalgic second, I envy the freckled and innocent children who grew up without television back in the days of fireside chats and *The Lone Ranger.* A group of students gathers near me on the balcony. The static rises. I jump onto a chair, lean toward the sky over the balcony's edge, and plug my free ear with a forefinger. For the next twenty minutes, I listen silently, straining from my awkward perch to hear every word.

On March 1, 2000, CNN and the *Los Angeles Times* are sponsoring a debate between Al Gore and Bill Bradley, the two candidates vying for the Democratic presidential nomination. These are debate negotiations. Negotiations precede all of the debates. Ed Reilly is the designated representative for the Bradley campaign. He is also a senior adviser with polish and a well-kept beard. The other participants descend from high levels to represent Time Warner, its affiliate CNN, the *Los Angeles Times,* and the Gore campaign. They are men and women of stature, significant men and women equipped to deal with vice presidents and senators.

I am a relative peon with no defensible role, no worthy title. Yet ever since the first Iowa debate back in January, Ed Reilly has asked me to phone in. When he is not available I contribute, but on these sorts of calls when he is at hand and the stakes are high, I rarely say a word. In fact, his reasons for including me are not altogether clear. I once thought that he wanted to make me more effective in my role as a Bradley advance person, but I have come to believe that he simply hopes to save himself the annoyance of having me phone him later for details.

The sponsors each have several representatives on the call, but a man from CNN with a smooth convincing voice speaks on behalf of them all. They are a unit, careful, clear, and united in their positions, unlike us, the two campaigns, forever clashing. The smooth-voiced spokesman from CNN summarizes the proposed format, which strictly parallels that of the last debate on February 21 at the Apollo Theatre in Harlem. It is our task during these conferences to determine the precise structure of the event. It is not boring. Actually, it is a little like watching surgery on television. It is a miraculous and daunting glimpse beneath the skin to the viscera of televised politics.

Having participated in several other debate formatting calls, I know what to expect. The two campaigns usually argue about the length of rebuttals. Thirty seconds are better for Bradley. Sixty seconds are better for Gore. Nobody ever says this, though. Instead, they argue with glossy motives and silvery civility about how the audience will benefit. They usually argue about the number of moderators, the size of the panels, and the value of closing statements. They have reasons for being exacting – well-plotted reasons – but these reasons, relating always to one candidate's strength or another's weakness, are hidden beneath a word or two about profiting the viewer. The producers usually mediate to their own advantage: They want something fast paced; they want so and so to moderate; they want no questions from the audience; they want questions from the audience. Everything is usually settled to the general discontent. I have an idea, though, that this call will be different, because the night before, our preliminary conference call ended abruptly, on a sour note, while I sat alone listening from the starchy white sheets of my bed in the Hollywood Roosevelt Hotel.

The spokesman from CNN finishes his overview and invites discussion. There is a pause, broken when the Gore representative, poised for action, states in feisty high-pitched tones that he is at a loss about where to begin because he objects to everything. The spokesman from CNN takes it in stride. He even offers a vote of confidence to the Gore representative: "Come, come, we know you'll choose just the right place to begin; we're certain of it." Some minutes pass, however, before it becomes clear to us that the Gore representative is concerned first and foremost about the broadcast hour, which has long been scheduled for six P.M. Pacific time, translating to nine P.M. eastern standard time. It may seem a trivial point, hardly worth noting, a bone for the dog, but not when taken in the appropriate context and eyed through the lens of national viewership.

Al Gore spent months publicly challenging Bill Bradley to a series of debates. The earliest of these challenges came in September, but the most memorable came during a debate on NBC's *Meet the Press*. It was December 19, 1999, and the two candidates sat side by side, within inches of each other, for sixty testy minutes.

"Let's debate twice a week from now until the nomination is decided and just go face-to-face about the issues and get rid of all these television and radio commercials. Why not do that?" Gore proposed.

"You know something? For the first ten months that I was running for president, you ignored me; you pretended I didn't exist. Suddenly I started to do better and you want to debate every day," Bradley replied. He then reminded Gore that they had been debating, that they had debated only two nights before, and that they would debate again several more times in January. Finally, he added with disdain, "The point is, Al, and I don't know if you get this, but a political campaign is not just a performance for people, which is what this is, but it is rather, a dialogue – "

"That's not what I am doing," Gore insisted, cutting Bradley off.

" – a dialogue with people," Bradley said, completing his thought.

"We could call this the *Meet the Press* agreement," Gore said. "We could have two debates every single week and get rid of all of the television and radio commercials. I'm willing to do it right now, if you're willing to shake on it." He held out his hand to Bradley.

Bradley, looking somewhat amused, declined: "Al, that's good. I like that hand. But the answer is no. I mean, why should I agree now? I'm not someone who's interested in tactics . . ."

"These aren't tactics," Gore objected, before continuing to push his point. "Look, I'm ready to agree right now."

"That's nothing but a ploy," Bradley said with a mixture of laughter and scorn.

"Debates aren't ploys," Gore maintained.

"No," Bradley replied, "to come here, shake my hand. That's nothing but a ploy."

Gore said that the American people deserved to hear a routine and elevated discussion of the issues and then made his proposal. Bradley refused the proposal, calling it transparent and gimmicky. He openly proclaimed that the enormous preparation required for such frequent debates would cut severely into other campaigning opportunities and that forsaking commercials would be a great and obvious misstep for him, a candidate with relatively low name recognition. He also suggested that the Gore campaign with their too quickly diminished funds were afraid to compete in the costly world of televised advertising. Gore ignored the accusations and continued to level challenges.

This dynamic began at a time when Bradley was still on the rise, when the gap between the two candidates was rapidly closing. The tides shifted, though, like the tides in the Bay of Fundy, with great speed and alarming volume. Gore regained momentum, and Bradley fell with gravity. Gore stopped making challenges and started avoiding debate commitments like the plague. Now, on this cold day in Los Angeles, the Gore representative is gloved to fight for a nine P.M. Pacific time broadcast, claiming that after catering over and over again to those on the East Coast, with East Coast debate after East Coast debate, he and his campaign plan to "respect the voters of California."

The spokesman from CNN listens to this argument and then points to the obvious, almost as if the obvious isn't obvious. The proposed shift in broadcast hour would dramatically restrict national viewership, insofar as a live broadcast in the East would then have to occur at midnight, long past prime time – past bedtime, for that matter. The proposed shift would exclude the possibility of a bicoastal audience, thereby eliminating half of the potential viewers. The spokesman from CNN favors a strict adherence to the original and long-established plan. To solidify his position, he offers statistics, pages and pages of hard, faxable statistics, which show that the Gore proposal would have an enormously negative effect on national viewer ratings while doing virtually nothing to improve the local ratings. In short, under no circumstances, none at all, would the sponsors concede the loss of national viewership or capital to the false notion that the voters of California would somehow feel slighted by a live six P.M. broadcast. Ed Reilly, our guy, the Bradley guy, presumed by all to be in favor of the original plan, is noticeably and contentedly silent.

Vainly the two sides argue, stating and restating the same points, as people often do in arguments until, after quite some time, the spokesman from CNN proposes a double airing. He is willing to broadcast the debate live at six P.M. in California as originally planned and then rebroadcast it again at nine P.M. to those same viewers. In theory, the Gore representative should accept the proposal. He wants a nine P.M. airing and has been offered a nine P.M. airing; but to the surprise of no one, he refuses it flatly. The proposal speaks to his stated objectives, not his underlying objectives, and the spokesman from CNN, clever man that he is, insists on contending with stated objectives. They are players strutting and fretting upon the stage, and the spokesman, not forgetting his part, asks for an explanation. "How in the world could you, emissary of the vice president, refuse a compromise that would prove so beneficial to the California audience after your heated and lengthy diatribes about pleasing the California audience?"

Ed Reilly, suddenly fed up, no longer willing to play the fool, interjects: "For Christ's sake, let's stop pretending. We all know that the voters of California aren't the issue. The Gore campaign would like nothing better than to have no debate at all, and if they can't get that, they'd like to limit the numbers of viewers to the greatest extent possible. When you are ahead, you avoid risks, and debating Bradley is a risk."

Of course, Ed Reilly is right. We all do indeed know that the voters of California are not the issue, but a decoy. At the moment, the Gore campaign's one and only concern is avoiding a nationally televised mishap or a last-minute Bradley knockout punch. Ed Reilly makes this point with calculated vehemence, in a manner befitting a skilled negotiator. I think of how my own voice might falter and leak. He reveals nothing more, nothing less, than desired. He is composed and civil. His tone is infused with humor and mockery. The humor lends him an air of confidence and superiority. The mockery conveys contempt but is too faint to warrant protest.

Ed Reilly's artful outburst is followed by a period of adjustment, with hemming and hawing from this corner and that. Before long, however, the Gore representative declares in no uncertain terms that Al Gore will not debate under these conditions. The words *will not debate* lie on the surface of my consciousness for two or three seconds before they become meaningful. Gore once spoke of "lifting up our democracy . . . with regular debates on the issues." He said, "Let's have one every week." He said it over and over. He even held out his hand to Bradley on national television and asked him to shake on it. Now, a manifest attempt first to downsize the audience, then to kill the debate entirely. It is hard for me to keep still, not to cackle or hoot, and harder yet to imagine a response to this unveiled threat.

The spokesman from CNN, the smooth and convincing spokesman, has the perfect response. Like a practiced poker player, even and temperate, invisibly elated, he calls the bluff and raises, asserting that Bradley will, if necessary, be put onstage with an empty chair. I want to clap, to jump up and down. I don't care that the spokesman's motives have nothing to do with mine, that his interest in reaching a national audience and preserving capital has nothing to with my interest in flinging this hypocrisy into the air like a kite.

Gleefully, I imagine an empty chair on national television for all to see, an empty chair onstage next to Bill Bradley under a spotlight for ninety priceless minutes, the perfect symbol of politics today. I imagine how awkward and funny it would be, almost like something dreamed up by a strange amalgam of Kafka and Russell Baker. I imagine all the jokes Bradley could make. "Well, Bernie [Bernard Shaw would be the moderator], I'd ask Al, but he's not here." There is roaring applause. Later in the show, Bradley turns to the empty chair as if to address Gore: "Whoops, I forgot, Al couldn't make it." I see headlines: SPARKS DON'T FLY AS BRADLEY DEBATES EMPTY CHAIR; EMPTY CHAIR SHARES GORE'S VISION FOR AMERICA'S FUTURE; AT STROKE OF MIDNIGHT, GORE LEAVES BEHIND EMPTY CHAIR, AMERICA IS LEFT TO WONDER ABOUT GLASS SLIPPER.

The Gore representative, acknowledging none of the humor or drama, suggests that the two campaigns take their candidates to a different network. He acts as though making a sudden ally of Bill Bradley's Ed Reilly is as sensible as an umbrella. I regress with the adolescent impulse to say in the snottiest and most sarcastic tone I can muster, "As if." Ed Reilly finds the proposal farfetched, too, chuckles even, and right then an image, the sort that has no obvious origin, flickers behind my closed eyelids. My father holds cards close to his chest while pushing a stack of poker chips toward me with a mischievous smile. Ed Reilly consents to arrange another debate at another hour on another network but apologetically refuses to rescind his commitment to this particular broadcast. The Gore representative hangs up, as does everyone else, with the understanding that a chair will be placed onstage and remain onstage for Gore's use up to the very last but that the show will go on with or without the opposing candidate.

Leak it to the press corps. Leak it to the press corps. I can think of nothing else as I lower myself from the chair. My legs tingle. *Who knows what evil lurks in the hearts of men?* I know, I think, as the line rattles through my head. Exhilarated and desperately tired, I look up and see in the curve of a gray cloud an ugly grimace. It is the face of realpolitik. I call Ed Reilly. He is hurried and impatient, indulging my outrage for only a moment.

"What happened to those debate challenges?" I ask. "I mean, this is hardly believable. It's one great big con. We can agree at least that this has nothing to do with principle or issues or anything high or good, can't we?"

I am almost begging. He excuses himself, giving me a verbal pat on the back. To him I am a child, one who should already know that Santa Claus isn't real. I drop the phone, feeling dizzy, as if I have bitten into a poison apple. I see scandal, but in an instant know that it will die with me. I am young, and somehow, in fate's curve, I have fallen into politics.

For six months the Bradley campaign employed me, and I

wandered, almost as an interloper, through the world of policy and principle, on the periphery of power, all the while forming a soft resolve to record the tale, mine and his. I don't think I was a cynic when I started and I don't think I am a cynic now, but somewhere in between I learned what it is to hate. There was a day or two when I hated indiscriminately, when just about everything appeared as a mean and foul obstacle to light and virtue. It was miserable to watch Bradley, the man I came to trust and love, fall in defeat and to feel my bones and coils fill with despair, the despair of watching another awful death.

My father died of pancreatic cancer in November 1994. I was, at twenty-one, his youngest child. He had ten children, related in varying degrees by a mixture of blood and marriage. Our family was an amalgam of families. My father's first marriage produced five children. My mother's first marriage produced four. Their marriages fell apart. They met. All nine children moved into one house, and then my parents had me.

When I was sixteen, my sister Sarah got married on the front lawn of our sprawling farm in New Jersey where the grass slopes down a long hill into a cornfield. Her guests walked through each other and the humid summer air onto the weeded bricks at the pool's edge, into the new red of the lawn furniture, up to the washed yellow of the tent, and onto the sanded brown of the dance floor. Bill Bradley was among these guests. He is writer John McPhee's close friend, and John, my mother's first husband, invited Bill to his daughter's wedding. Towering above the others on the lawn, he, our senator, added to the buzz of music, chiming champagne glasses, and rising laughter. Later, as the others started purring with alcohol and as the yellow sun turned to orange, the orange to red, and the red to purple, he walked across the lawn onto the hard black of the basketball court.

Most people saw a New Jersey senator and a New York Knick standing among them, but I saw the young, almost unnaturally disciplined athlete of John's book *A Sense of Where You Are*. I had recently read this account of Bill Bradley's early basketball career and could not stem my envy for the boy who practiced four and five hours a day, who practiced not only out of love but also out of a sense of competition, never intending to lose to an opponent who had devoted more time to honing skills. With something greater than a child's focus and just a little less than Simone Weil's saintly masochism, Bradley would dribble, wearing plastic glasses that prevented him from looking down, and put weights in his shoes to improve his vertical leap. By the time he graduated from Princeton University, he had a perfect sense of where he was on the court and could shoot from almost anywhere with his eyes closed. Unnatural or not, this impressed me, also an athlete, but an athlete who threw a baseball for eight hours in one day after first signing up for Little League and then let the glove gather dust, who dribbled until her hand ached upon falling in love with Isaiah Thomas's smile, only to then become enraptured with mastering Pelé's bicycle kick.

I didn't think at a happy sixteen to consider whether it was the politician, the man, or the guest who allowed himself to be led, suit and all, onto the hot asphalt where my brothers and I stood with a basketball. After slipping off my shoes and bunching up my bridesmaid dress, I tried not to smile too brightly when he took me as a partner. The large orange ball looked small in his hands, and each time he shot, it followed the same elegant arc into our tilted basket. His passes came like tiny tastes of wedding cake, and my own shots – a few, at least – lumbered heavily through the rim to the sound of my brothers' joyful whoops. At the end, he took a small bucket of blue paint brought perhaps by my father and wrote, on the basketball court, "Joan and Bill, 1990."

In August 1999, I remember that wedding day as National Public Radio draws a picture, glorious and hopeful, of Bill Bradley's 2000 presidential campaign. I am a civil servant employed by a city agency. I dress for work in front of a fan, sweating in the summer heat, and think of the book I have just begun reading, *The Education of Henry Adams*, and in an adult version of trying to learn Pelé's bicycle kick, I resolve on getting an education in politics.

With a practical and imaginative journey into a new realm as my dream and an erosion of my ideals as my fear, I send a letter and résumé to the Bill Bradley headquarters in West Orange, New Jersey. A week later, a brusque woman with a high-pitched voice calls to ask if I am interested in compliance, field, or fund-raising. She assumes that I understand what working in these departments would entail. She is also occupied with a number of other simultaneous conversations, and in all of them, her tone is marked by fatigue and anxiety. She clearly has no time for explanations. I am left to make three quick, baseless decisions on my own. Fund-raising could be done anywhere and would fall far short of providing the education I envision. Compliance is in some way connected to campaign finance reform, a topic of supreme importance, and might prove interesting. Field is at the core of all things political and should be pursued.

Compliance calls first, and in a light grayish green suit, bearing some resemblance to the suits worn by Dana Scully of *The X-Files*, I take a bus through the slums of Newark to the isolated offices of Bradley's campaign headquarters. A clean-cut man with a bottomless smile meets me and shows me a maze of whitewashed hallways leading from frenetic department to frenetic department. Boxes fill the corners and seams of every haphazard room, clipped articles intermingled with maps and candidate photos litter the meandering walls, and makeshift desks leak computer cords and loose papers until the entire building seems to sink in a flood of chaos. The young, casually dressed inhabitants of this world betray, with their pale skin and softened bodies, the hours and months spent dutifully occupied in this suburban box. They smile, though, with no discernible longing for the pause of sacrificed weekends, and the corrosive effect politics poses to principle dims briefly in my mind.

The clean-cut man stops when the maze of hallways brings us to the compliance department. A candy given to me by the receptionist, quite forgotten and never wanted, becomes sticky and soft in my closed palm, and I sit clenching my fist to contain it. At length, he asks about my interest in working for Bill Bradley, and as I respond with premeditated and deliberate words, all of which are true, a sense of shame fills me.

"I've spent the last two and a half years working for the New York City Civilian Complaint Review Board as an investigator of police misconduct." I start with facts but then launch into something more akin to lofty purpose. "I initially accepted the position with an eye more toward public service than city politics, but the agency, still in its infancy and the subject of debate and controversy, is a political one, very much defined by politics and politicians. In any case, civil service with its daily exposure to the community and city government has been more satisfying and valuable than I ever anticipated."

"Uh-huh." He leans forward in a polite gesture of interest.

Trying to maintain eye contact and with the words *satisfying and valuable* echoing painfully in my right eardrum, I continue. "Now that I am ready to make a career change and know that politics and public service are inextricably linked, I can think of nothing more alluring than the prospect of working for Bill Bradley in his bid for the presidency." I wonder if stripping would be any more humiliating.

"Why Bill Bradley?" Each syllable is cheerful.

"I grew up in New Jersey with Bill Bradley as my senator and in the Princeton area with him as an athletic and political mentor. I also majored in American studies with a concentration in African American studies and feel compelled by his emphasis on racial understanding."

"We love people who love Bradley." His eyes brighten.

"But, more important than anything, I guess, is the fact that in Bill Bradley, a politician who appears far less partisan and far more idealistic than most, I see potential for renewed faith in the political process." My clothes loosen as the sound of each unoriginal word, *mentor, compelled,* and *renewed,* slips off my tongue and deflates my very figure. The clean-cut man's smile remains bottomless.

15

It should be easy for me to talk to him about Bradley. I have been following his campaign pretty closely. I wouldn't consider entering politics for another soul, but certain truths in certain hands have a trite ring. In my hands, truth says that Bradley is a beacon of hope in dark domain. He wants to liberate our democracy from the tyranny of dollar-driven politics. He wants to eliminate child poverty, register and license all handguns, and give every American access to health care. He wants to tap our hidden streams of morality and do bold things, and I want to help him. He is a man schooled in practical politics who believes still that idealism is more than a mere word. At a time of political farce and pandemonium, he not only announced that politics is broken, he also relinquished his senatorial office, which seemed to say that it is power's potential, not plain power, that he is after. In a world where morality can be as politically precarious as crime, he shows courage. He is a good man, an honest man, and I believe that we would serve ourselves well by electing him to office. That is truth in my hands with its trite ring. Also in my hands is a piece of melting candy.

Compliance, I discover, is the art of creating paperwork to document campaign contributions and the art of summarizing that documentation in lengthy reports submitted to the Federal Election Commission and the general public. The compliance staff serves as the campaign's accountants, and by keeping the money honest, they contribute to the integrity of Bill Bradley's campaign finance reform platform. They have, however, no charming or academic connection to this essential issue, and as I leaf through a copy of their most recent quarterly report, finding page upon page of numbers without words, my face droops. Watching me, the clean-cut man explains that his ultimate concern is more with getting good people involved than with meeting the particular needs of his department. He doesn't know what other openings there are within the campaign but gives me an idea of where I might look.

"Research is in the business of research," he chuckles without a hint of cynicism. He can't say exactly what the department researches, the candidate himself, perhaps, but it sounds like interesting business to him. The department retains, though, an aura of exclusivity that discourages friendly inquiry. "Issues, politics, scheduling, fund-raising, and press do just what you might guess," he says. The difference between issues and politics would be rather difficult to guess, I think, but dismiss the subject as he begins explaining advance. He has just gone down to Crystal City, Missouri, to help the advance team with the campaign kickoff. "The job is exciting," he says, "but the pressure of putting together high-profile events for the candidate with all sorts of sudden and arbitrary objectives falling on top of you from who knows where was just too much, more than I could handle, anyway."

The clean-cut man smiles good-bye, and I depart for the Civilian Complaint Review Board, which on my arrival seems strangely subdued. The walls look emptier and the investigative case files look neater than before. I sit at my desk, take off my jacket, and relax with the thought that no one can reject me from a job I don't want. The risk gone, I decide to tell my girlfriend, who is a lawyer and who also happens to work right down the hall from me, about the interview.

"Politics? Huh," she says after draining the remains from a can of Diet Coke.

"What?" I ask, suddenly irritated.

"I'm just surprised. Since when are you interested in politics? You don't even read the paper." There is an edge to her voice.

"I read the paper," I say, standing just inside her office door as she sits ten feet away behind her desk.

"OK, but you don't know who Dan Rather is." Her arms are crossed, and her suit looks especially dark. "You've never watched *Larry King Live*, let alone a serious political show."

"Who cares what I watch? It doesn't have anything to do with it. I see a chance to get an education, that's all." For the first time, it occurs to me that there is something odd about my choosing politics. Then again, politics is only part of it. I also want to move on from this job, my first out of college, and, as if it is possible, to escape the anxiety I feel about the future by doing something new, something with unknown possibilities.

"I expected you to move into the arts or publishing or something," she continues.

"I work here, don't I? How is investigating police misconduct a predictable or logical choice?" I ask. "Anyway, it's just an interview. I'm sure nothing will come of it."

Almost as soon as I return to my desk, the Bradley campaign's Iowa field director, Pete D'Allessandro, calls. He has the voice of a man on the far end of an ugly caffeine high but speaks with a familiarity that puts me at ease. He introduces himself, saying he played a large role in Governor Vilsack's unexpected victory, duped the powers-that-be into thinking he is a capable organizer, and ended up in charge of the Iowa field operation. With my girlfriend's earlier comment about Dan Rather jumping from my memory, I wonder if Vilsack is a name I should recognize. Pete D'Allessandro then mutters something about how he probably doesn't know as many words as a Yale graduate but is a good boss and an athlete, too, not an all-American athlete like me, but an athlete. He claims that in researching me on the Internet, he found an impressive set of senior-year lacrosse statistics. Hardly believing that any such information about me is available and not sure why he would choose to research it, I am silent. With no other prelude, he makes a job offer.

I would work in Polk County, unless I want to be sent out to the cornfields, but he thinks Polk County, home to Des Moines, would best suit me, a New Yorker. His voice races with fatigue, and I imagine the ends of his hair to be slightly wet with perspiration. My days would consist of tiers, precincts, door knocking, public addresses, phone banking, and caucus night planning. He could pay me $1,700 a month, which would include housing, but I would need to bring my own car, for which I would be paid twenty-five cents on the mile. Having only a foggy idea what it all means, but reluctant to reveal my ignorance and steal time from a man who no doubt is responsible for the phones ringing at his side, I ask nothing further. By Friday he needs an answer, and work would have to begin no later than October 4, which is only two weeks away.

My suit attracts attention that day, and not because it reminds people of Dana Scully. I have never worn a suit to work before. I also arrived a few hours late, and my colleagues, all of them

19

investigators, know enough to guess that I have been to an interview. I brush off most of their inquiries with quips and evasive smiles, but I offer one investigator, who is particularly astute and also trustworthy, an explanation. As it turns out, he has a friend in Iowa working for Bill Bradley. He puts me in touch with this friend, Gabe Lazarus, a member of the advance team, who then puts me in touch with the national advance director, who is hiring. And it just so happens that another member of the advance team, at the time consisting of only six people, is Megan Hall.

Megan is close to my best friend's sister, so I know of her. We speak and she gives me her impressions, which are useful on their own, but when I learn how much we have in common, it seems a foregone conclusion, almost like a beckoning from beyond, that our paths will cross again. She is not only close to my best friend's sister, but also played lacrosse against me in college, dated the first boy I ever loved, and left a girlfriend behind in New York to work for Bill Bradley in Iowa. That is the progress of the day, and from then until my arrival in Des Moines, I tuck and roll through one long somersault of decision and drama, which causes an arresting pain to shoot chronically up my neck and into the back of my brain.

In a book called *Travels with Charley,* John Steinbeck wrote, "A projected journey spawns advisors in schools." Megan Hall, perhaps the most valuable of my spawned advisers, thinks advance is the better choice. She agrees that there are more substantive aspects to fieldwork – namely, learning the issues and immersing yourself in local politics – but finds the best part of her days are spent seeing Bill Bradley in action.

Megan is in a car when we speak, on her way to meet Bill Bradley at the airport, having spent the earlier portion of her day searching for event sites in small New Hampshire counties. As an advance person, responsible primarily for building events and moving the candidate, she sees a lot of Bradley. I am charmed by what rises in my imagination. I picture myself wandering about the countryside choosing quirky and novel locations for grand and heroic events and then dashing off to meet and escort the esteemed senator.

Other advisers, ones with hardening political experience, bring forth pictures not as rosy. They fear that I will hate advance. It attracts, they say, ambitious young politicos vying relentlessly for time with the candidate. They characterize advance people as student government types who smoke pot but cautiously forbid anyone from photographing them in the act for fear of jeopardizing their political futures. I am reminded of a guy in college who, realizing that a photograph had already been taken, removed and destroyed the roll of film from the offending camera. He was a well-spoken, promising young man with an interest in music, but he hated rock concerts because rock concerts forced him to brush shoulders with "undesirables."

My impulse suddenly is to shy away not only from advance but also from politics. I sway back and forth like a porch swing, influenced as easily as a small child. I don't have much relevant experience of my own through which to filter these opinions, and when it comes to the mechanics of our political system, I know close to nothing. This compounds the strain and bareness of deciding so abruptly to drop everything familiar and move to Iowa.

The pragmatic advisers, my girlfriend among them, believe that advance will leave me better situated than field if Bradley becomes president. He will recognize me, know me, and even trust me when the time comes for filling the coveted White House positions. It is difficult for me to concede that this is a meaningful point, and I deny coveting a position in the White House, but I listen. I listen too as my girlfriend explains why Iowa is a state of such political importance.

"You mean you don't know?" she asks.

It does not surprise her in the least, but she enjoys teasing, and it amuses her greatly to think of me running off to Iowa when I cannot even define a caucus. (Later, she will give me *The Almanac of American Politics 2000*, a heavy book decorated with an American flag.)

"That's right, I don't know." It is sometimes nice to be teased.

"Well, have you ever heard of the Iowa caucuses?"

"All right, all right, go ahead."

Iowa has caucuses instead of a primary, she explains. Caucuses are different from primaries. In Iowa, people don't go to the polls to vote for their party's nominee, they go to meetings where they discuss, deliberate, and then choose a candidate from among the nominees. The media pay very close attention to Iowa's caucuses because its caucuses begin the presidential selection process, because its caucuses come before any other state's primary or caucuses. In fact, the media use them as a sort of bellwether and, on the basis of the results, make predictions that influence everything to follow. My girlfriend thinks it is a terrible system. She speaks at some length about how Iowa, an entirely unrepresentative state, without big cities, urban areas, or minority populations, should not wield such power and about how only party regulars and party activists end up voting. She then quizzes me on the branches of government and the names of prominent senators, which for her somehow lightens the prospect of my leaving for such a long and indeterminate period of time.

I listen when the national advance director, arguing also along lines of pragmatism, suggests that after Iowa, as media campaigning becomes the dominant force, field-workers will lose their value and be shifted to other departments, while I, having established myself in advance, would be traveling all over the country. I listen too as a close friend expresses fear that she will lose the one remaining idealist in her life if I fly off to this world I know not of. I listen as my family indulges fanciful dreams about my helping Bill Bradley cure the world's evils. I listen as my colleagues talk of running into me at an airport six months or a year down the road. They say that I will be wearing a suit; have a cell phone in my hand, a laptop at my side, and Secret Service men in tow; and be rushing off to some important meeting. I listen as shiftless, contented advisers warn against the long hours and endless weeks.

Eventually I call Pete D'Allessandro, the Iowa field director, and confess my dilemma. He says that "choosing advance over field would be like applying for a demotion." He doesn't have time to feign objectivity. He tells me that either way I will have to decide soon, in the next day or two, because he is in no position to wait. I begin soliciting advice. I call John McPhee, father to four of my sisters, a person to whom I turn periodically for certain types of guidance. He suggests that if, in the end, I like politics, I can always revisit it and try fieldwork, but that the opportunity to see and know a great leader like Bill Bradley might never come again.

I choose advance because of this final advice, because I believed Megan when she said that watching Bill Bradley is the best part of her job, because I want to travel after Iowa, and because the clean-cut man with the bottomless smile made, with his admonitions, advance seem exciting.

All sorts of questions remain: ones of critical depth and bearing, ones of little meaning, ones that might never be answered. The questions are speckled and assorted. They are stock and spare, bleak and impossible. The questions fly and whiz, even as that pain shoots up my neck and into the back of my brain. First I ask, "Am I crazy to hope?" Finally I ask, "Can there be any expectation of return?" In between, I ask everything from "Why was I hired?" to "Where will he land?" I make a leap of faith with these questions in waiting and hold, all the while, a small, entirely private wish that he and I will one day find ourselves together again on a basketball court.

2

Frivolous Indignities

Whoever fights monsters should see to it that in the process
he does not become a monster. And when you look long into
an abyss, the abyss also looks into you.

—Friedrich Nietzsche

THE WHEELS HIT the runway with a muted thump. I
have landed next to a long, low strip mall in the heart of the
Midwest. A heated desire to go toward something new brings me
here. It is the vast, vague potential that I love. A chance to know the
world more fully came at me, and I lurched forward with it, lured
by a tall man with tall and beautiful ideals. I left everything behind,
including fear. I have feared, in these years just after college, not
knowing where to go or what I like or how to love. I left behind a
small two-bedroom brownstone apartment with redbrick walls and
a broken marble fireplace. I left a dangerous and invigorating habit
of Rollerblading to work over the Brooklyn Bridge, along the busy
streets of lower Manhattan. I left a job that led me into the briny
deeps of the outer boroughs, through the assorted lives of officers
and their alleged victims. I left a girlfriend with truth at the core of
her soul, who is forlorn at my absence but generous with her
support. I left a family surging with contagious drama. I brought

one black-and-white photograph of my father grinning from the driver's seat of his first car. He is a boy in the 1940s, no more than fifteen, skinny, handsome, and full of glee. As we amble off the plane, I try to imagine what he would say if he were alive. I would like to hear him tell me what a brave and good girl I am. I would like to hear his farfetched and fabulous plans for my future in the White House, as the secretary of education, as the redeemer of politics.

The terminal's corridor is wide and empty. New York's La Guardia Airport, full of flutter and bustle, seems very far away, much farther away than our winged leap could have taken us. I don't know when or how or even if I will return. The other passengers look as though they have returned already, as though Iowa is home. I peek into a small gift shop and find it filled with cornfield postcards, porcelain hogs, and speckled gray Iowa State University T-shirts.

A young man, not more than twenty-five, with closely cropped hair, big ears, and a solid figure, walks toward the new arrivals. His sense of purpose makes him stand out. Here, in the Des Moines Airport, his quick pace has something of the outsider about it. He passes me, then turns to look. In a flash, I see myself through his eyes: short dark hair, a slender boyish manner, a pretty feminine face, and a grave expression.

"You must be Joan," he says.

I smile, trying my best to seem friendly, knowing that he will think me serious and aloof in these first moments.

His name is Gabe Lazarus. This is the Gabe who put me in touch with the national advance director. He arranges for my car rental while I collect my bags: one large blue canvas duffel bag and one brand-new hanging suitcase for my brand-new suits. I follow him to my apartment building, a mile or so down the road, found for me by the campaign. Gabe wants me to leave my car in the parking lot there and ride with him. It will make things easier and more efficient. Efficiency bursts from his seams.

The building is boxy, three-story, paper-thin public housing surrounded by tarmac, right off the highway's edge. Gabe waits in the car while I take my things inside and change clothes. I move slowly toward the flimsy broken glass of the lobby door. It has no lock. Rows of apartments line the sides of the long, straight institutional hallway. There is a stale, pungent odor, an unsanitary version of the odor in my grandmother's nursing home. The key given to me by Gabe, given to Gabe by my new roommate, Allison Dobson, rattles in the keyhole of my ground-level apartment, and I push open the door.

The living room has grimy tan carpeting that creeps from whitewashed wall to whitewashed wall. The ceiling is low. A sliding glass door is at the far end of the room. Thin vertical cuts of plastic form a blind. Through the broken and missing pieces, I see the decaying side of an identical building. Trees are not visible; neither is grass. A chocolate brown couch sits against the near wall. There are no lamps, no posters, no coffee tables, no books, nothing, not a single personal item. In fact, the only other objects in the room are a radio and an ironing board. In the kitchen, I find a bare card table without chairs. The first bedroom I pass belongs to Allison. I am relieved to spot, through the open door, a clutter of clothing, toiletries, drawings, and photographs. In my room, a double bed sits under a polyester comforter across from a dresser with a glossy faux wood finish. The mattress collapses beneath my weight. I would rest for a few minutes, weary as I am, but the opportunity to reflect seems menacing. I change into more professional clothing as Gabe advised, lock the door behind me, and hope that a strong wind will come and blow the building to Kansas.

Gabe is on his cell phone when I get into his green Chevy Lumina. He hops to another call as we pull away and still another as we head onto the interstate. He has not yet told me where we are going. His beeper sounds. He pulls it off his belt, hangs up on the person he is speaking to, and returns the page. I get a teasing, prodding urge to ask why he has both a beeper and a cell phone, but I say nothing, fearing that he will take it in the wrong spirit and that my aversion to it all will be seen and resented.

We stop at a warehouse with orange corrugated siding in a deserted neighborhood on the outskirts of town. We have an appointment to see podiums. We need an easygoing podium, the sort that won't look out of place among the tractors or in front of the abandoned hog run on the Dunn family farm, where Bradley will speak in a few days. A salesman wearing a tie and short-sleeved shirt leads us to an upstairs room, almost like an attic, with a strange array of objects buried in dust and strewn in the most haphazard of fashions. He pulls forward three podiums. Gabe dismisses the first two handily. The third he considers, then decides that it needs a thinner stem and a more natural finish. A feeling like the one I used to get in museums as a child passes over me, bringing fatigue and thoughts of other places: playing fields, picnics, and swimming pools.

In the ten days leading up to my October 4 departure, I did nothing but rush frantically about, completing and organizing all that I could at my office, packing my belongings, searching for someone to sublet my apartment, and saying good-bye at each open interval. I hardly slept. I even attended a friend's wedding in Martha's Vineyard the weekend before my departure.

Getting to the island, off the coast of Massachusetts, on a Friday after my last day of work and back in time for my eight A.M. Monday morning flight would have been difficult on its own, but there was more. My girlfriend, Flo, had not originally intended to come, but when the weekend turned into my last two days on the planet, we rearranged. Instead of flying, we drove, and the drive was slow. We almost missed the ferry, arrived too late for the rehearsal dinner, and found that the house we had arranged to stay in was locked.

The memories come unbidden as I wait about for Gabe to collect suggestions from the salesman on where to find other podiums. Flo and I fought at the wedding. She, formerly a prosecutor, believes in the justice system. I believe in mitigating circumstances, that criminals often as not are victims and that the prison system is a dynamo out of whack, beyond control. We argued with vehemence, more like devils than devil's advocates, as though mercy and punishment, not my impending departure, were the points of greatest tension.

It is now noonish, and I am in an orange warehouse in Des Moines searching for the perfect podium, wondering if Gabe would sympathize with my fatigue. We leave the warehouse and get back on the highway. I ask Gabe if he is hungry. He looks surprised and then, realizing that it is lunchtime, tells me that he knows a place where we can grab a bite. He finishes almost as soon as the plate is placed in front of him and stands up to leave, but I have not yet begun. My soup is still steaming. Reluctantly, he sits back down. I begin to wonder if everyone on the Bradley campaign will look conservative and burst with efficiency.

The Jefferson-Jackson Day Dinner, referred to as "the JJ Dinner," is the big upcoming event, the reason I was flown out here in a hurry. I learn that all sorts of helpers and advisers are being flown out in a hurry. The event, only a few days away, is the biggest Democratic fund-raiser of the season, held in the Des Moines convention center and hosted by the Iowa Democratic Party, the IDP. It will bring the first joint appearance of Bill and Al, Bradley and Gore, the senator and the vice president, our candidate and their candidate.

People take their pick between name and title depending on how they are viewed and how they view themselves. I find the matter a puzzle, a bit irksome even, and hearing Gabe call Bradley "the senator," as he has done several times in the last few minutes while talking on his cell phone, makes me think of a scene in *Anna and the King*, a silly remake of *The King and I*, a movie that I saw somewhere, on a plane, perhaps. Jodie Foster, a widowed English-woman, travels to Thailand in the mid–nineteenth century to serve as governess to the king's children. Servants, relatives, wives, and counselors alike fall to their knees when the king enters, bowing their heads deeply, never daring to look up – but not Jodie Foster, who, as the king later comments, considers herself not only the equal of a man, but also the equal of a king.

My parents always encouraged my friends to address them not as Mr. and Mrs., but as Dan and Pryde. It made me proud to have such parents. Children take pride in odd things. I was proud to have big hands and to have once eaten thirteen ears of corn. When my mother said to my tiny schoolmate, "Please call me Pryde," or when my father said in his rich Texan accent, "My name is Dan," I was also proud. If I had thought about it, I might have understood that I liked the idea of everyone, regardless of age, rank, or title, starting as equals. I might also have understood that I liked the idea of having unconventional parents.

As a child, I saw equality as good and everything opposing it as bad. I now see that government buildings are constructed with gilded domes, lofty ceilings, and vast halls to evoke awe because governing bodies in order to be fully effective must have the respect of the citizenry. Architecture is a means to an end. In the same way, I see how a man running for president benefits from titles. My mind wanders here during lunch while Gabe talks on his cell phone, and I resolve vaguely to be reverent with resolve that is weakened, by pride and principle of the simplest kind, almost as soon as it is born.

After lunch, Gabe and I whip by Iowa headquarters, too chockfull for my immediate absorption, except I note a great buzz of activity, a total absence of windows, and a coffeemaker in the bathroom. My roommate, Allison, gives me a brief warm welcome and dashes apologetically back to her duties at a desk among lots of other desks with a phone and a map of Iowa, which is pierced by a colorful assortment of thumbtacks. Gabe and I then race off to the airport to collect a man whom Gabe humbly refers to as "the advance guru."

Mullen – by birthright Eric Mullen, but people in advance, especially those of Mullen's ilk, are often called by their last names is – young to be a guru. He is in his late twenties, only a few years older than me, younger than he looks owing to the balding and the belly, but attractive nonetheless. He bursts with confidence and big ideas the way Gabe bursts with efficiency. I alternate between preferring confidence to efficiency, efficiency to confidence, but by the end of the weekend have a distinct preference for efficiency because I find, at least in the case of Gabe, that it is attended by hard work.

Mullen takes a front seat in Gabe's rental. I withdraw to the back, wrap an arm around a bent knee, and rest my forehead against the cool glass of the window. Gabe fiddles with the radio.

"So you know Carson?" Mullen's inquiry has a chummy quality to it.

"Oh yeah, Jay was out here for a long time before he went to California." Gabe is respectful, deferential even.

"Carson was a rookie on the Schumer campaign, a talented rookie, who did all sorts of crazy things. After a few months of me teaching him the ropes, that kid was top of the line, cream of the crop," Mullen boasts. "So you have Carson's number?" He expects yes for an answer and gets it.

Mullen removes his cell phone, which hangs loosely from a clasp on his belt, and calls Carson. "What's your twenty?" he asks. I gather that twenty means location in Mullen- or advance-speak, because Mullen then comments that the sunny Los Angeles shores must suit Carson.

Eventually Mullen turns to me. "So, what about you? When did your go wheels down?"

"Excuse me?" I don't immediately understand his meaning.

"When did you land?"

"Today, just a few hours ago, not long before you."

"Welcome." Mullen turns to Gabe with a smirk.

I have so little to stand on, am so vulnerable in my newness, that Mullen's mentoring tone grates on me. Yet I am curious. I want to know more about him. "How did you get involved in politics?" I ask.

He tells me that he visited Washington, D.C., at seventeen with his parents, fell in love, not with the women but with Capitol Hill, and never left. He went to college nearby, working for politicians straight through, and now, after serving as Senator Charles Schumer's deputy chief of staff, is the founder and chief executive officer of his own political consulting firm. He also tells me that he has done advance work for every living president.

"What did you think of Reagan?" I am again curious.

He looks at me with surprise and contempt, as if to say, How big an idiot could you be? and sputters a "Well, not Reagan" response of some kind. I resist asking what he meant by "every living president."

We return to Iowa headquarters, which I now notice is on a wide street called University Avenue in a flat, humorless building containing a video store, a cellular phone outlet, and a pizza restaurant, all chains, all with awful fluorescent lighting. Headquarters is wedged back between the pizza and cellular phones in a single room, a sort of storage space, no larger than a midsize swimming pool. Across the street is a shopping center, and Mullen drags me there on a whim, something the focused Gabe cannot do, busy as he is. To my relief, I find that Mullen has a sense of fun, and for a moment, the first moment since my arrival, I relax. He wants to buy a toothbrush and candy, lots and lots of candy. He has been trying desperately to lose weight but can't resist Twizzlers, bite-size Snickers, or Blow Pops.

"What do you want?" he asks generously after pulling several bags off the shelf.

I pause before answering. "I don't really eat candy, but thanks."

He gives me a probing look. Then, as if sensing some quirk of character, he asks, "What else don't you eat?"

"I have never had a soda." I shrug and smile, anticipating his surprise.

"What? Were you homeschooled or something?"

"Actually, I have never had much of a sweet tooth, and bubbles have always hurt my mouth." I consider leaving it at that but then confess, "As a child, I probably also took pleasure in the approving looks that this information – that is, not liking soda – elicited from adults."

When we return to headquarters, Gabe makes it my task to find the podium. Mullen pipes in, asking how tall the senator is, and like a kid in class, I reply that he is six feet five. Mullen then says, quite seriously, "Well, it will have to be a tall podium, won't it?" Gabe looks at Mullen with considerable awe and goes on to explain how it can't be showy or shine too much. A light unfinished wood would be best, he says. With a phone book in one hand and Gabe's notes in the other, I start to make calls, ill at the thought of spending the next six months looking for podiums, woefully remembering all that I left behind. I identify four vendors that carry podiums and set out in Gabe's car, relieved to be on my own, happy to decide the pace.

The first podium is a massive dark object laminated with peeling sheets of plastic, recognizable only because of the large metal gooseneck bolted to the top. I drive elsewhere. This place gave me a description over the phone of a podium that sounded just right, but now they don't know where that podium is, can't find it anywhere, will I please forgive them? I head to another spot, which has two podiums, one with a very odd internal speaker system projecting out from it like a goiter and the other fancy enough for an inaugural address. I will save this second one until after Bradley gets elected, I think playfully as I inspect its gaudy and ornate lines. The last location, a hotel, has lots of podiums, more than you could ever want, all identical, all wrapped in thick off-white carpeting.

I return to headquarters. Most of the activity and discussion concerns the JJ Dinner. The dinner is set to occur before an important partisan crowd of two or three thousand. And because Iowa is home to the first voting of the season, because Gore and Bradley will be appearing together for the first time in this ever tightening race, a fairly large media presence is expected. The event is taken seriously. The trouble is that the Iowa Democratic Party made a lot more tickets available to the Gore campaign than to us, effectively guaranteeing that we will be soundly outnumbered at this nationally televised affair. In creative retaliation, our campaign decided to have its own event, an alternative event, to let the world know that people are banging down the doors to show their support for Bill Bradley.

This alternative event will occur at the same time as the JJ

Dinner in a building right across the street. Entertainers with big names, politicians with big voices, and celebrities of great renown will attend to lend suitable luster. Without this alternative event, the headline would be, or so it is believed, something to the effect of GORE DEVOTEES, OUT IN SCORES, DROWN MEAGER GATHERING OF BRADLEY FOLLOWERS. The story would, of course, fail to acknowledge the bias of structure, the heavily weighted ticket distribution. This is what Gabe tells me, anyway, and he seems reasonable, but I remind myself, as if it is possible, to differentiate between what I know and what I have been told. He tells me that there was never even a pretense to equal opportunity. He doesn't need to tell me that Bradley is up against entrenched power, against a man who has the president of the United States standing loyally at his side. I know from following the campaign, from reading the newspapers, that Bradley's court of appeal, to paraphrase Pulitzer Prize-winning journalist, Theodore White, will have to be the people, that he will have to look over the heads of the politicians and show strength in the community and later at the polls.

Late in the afternoon, a small group of Bradley staff, including Gabe, Mullen, and me, gather in the Capitol Square Atrium, the site of the alternative event, to consider the space. Gabe has been there many times to map it all out, to develop a plan. He knows where the banners will go and how they will be hung, where the food will be served and who will serve it, where the holding rooms are and what VIPs will be held in them. He knows where the stage will stand and who will stand on it. He knows when the radios are being delivered and who is delivering them. He knows it all, but I, not yet invested and not yet needed, have a difficult time caring and have just as difficult a time imagining how all these inane details can be so very riveting to those around me.

Mullen digs right in, adopting his consultant role with great flair, throwing terms about, testing Gabe, and making suggestions. I start paying attention when he asks if there will be veterans and if we can get them close to the stage, if there will be children, old people, or "folks" in wheelchairs. If veterans can't be guaranteed, he wants American flags, lots of them. This is par for the course, I tell myself, but can't help marveling at what a crass business it all is.

By the end of the week, I am ready to go home. I hate buying diet grape soda, Diet Sunkist, and strange flavors of Gatorade, "the senator's" preferred beverages. I hate it because, while there is nothing else to ground me, I feel degraded. Besides, I wish the guy would drink fruit juice or something. In fact, despite Gabe's admonitions, I throw in a few small cans of V8 and a few small bottles of apple, orange, and cranberry juice, hoping that he will be tempted. Diet grape and orange soda are the favorites, though, and must be placed in the back of Bradley's vehicle, along with carrots and bananas, low-calorie items for a man worried about his profile.

I hate the building where I live, which never blows to Kansas, and loathe going home at night, even though I am always tired. The odor in the hallways becomes so offensive to me that I find and use a long, roundabout route to a side entrance nearer my own door. I hate the food, dread each meal: hard, strange-textured bagels for breakfast, thick, meaty sandwiches topped with opaque lettuce for lunch, and chicken fingers for dinner. I search for, without finding, a decent diner where I can get fried eggs and bacon for breakfast on the occasional morning when it is still early and I am in no great rush. The tourist pamphlet I pick up and read in hopes of discovering something more lists Domino's Pizza as one of the five recommended Italian restaurants in town.

I hate the hours, the mind-set. We get to the office at nine in the morning and rarely let off before eleven or twelve at night, busying ourselves with things like driving directions, which require the recording of exact times and the measuring of exact distances, and with renting vehicles roomy enough for our candidate, the man with long, long legs. Mullen, who moves in and out of sternness, sternly advises that we should refer to Bill Bradley not by name, but as "our candidate," so that when we mention him in restaurants where, unknown to us, eavesdroppers lurk, we won't attract attention, no one will know of whom we speak. It strikes me as silly pretension, part of Mullen's pomp and play at power. Yet I can't help wondering if, at some point, I will be a subscriber, if all that I see and criticize will became a part of me. Still, the days seem unnecessarily long. My colleagues spend sixteen hours at the office out of habit more than anything else, because, or so it seems, nothing outside our campaign interests them anymore, here in this foreign environment where work, love, and life are all bound into one.

I should long since have called home to tell them that I arrived safely but would rather not share these frivolous indignities with my sister Jenny, the single biggest proponent of my coming out here, or with my mother, who fears always for my happiness. I would rather not tell them that I left a deep and absorbing job, one where I had authority and input, in order to be a gofer, to fetch soda and probe for podiums. How do I admit to them, when I can't admit to myself, that I feel superior to this, that my talents are being wasted? How do I tell them that I hate the city, the food, my apartment, and this awful, crass business? How do I tell them that I have spent a good portion of every day wanting to cry?

Harder and stranger still, though it is clear that my colleagues are sincere and avid Bradley supporters, politics is little discussed. In my preliminary musings, I saw a dreamy glow around men and women transfixed by ideas. I expected at least a few long nights of the talk and argument that inform opinion and shape thought, but it is almost as though politics is beside the point. In fact, I often have the feeling that this is the most conservative lot of people I have ever worked with and find it baffling.

Mullen is hardly representative of the campaign – just a political consultant out for a long weekend – but he certainly doesn't allow loyalty for Bradley to have undue effect. I get the idea that he would work for just about anybody. He is not sure which candidate he will vote for, or so he says, although if I had to wager, I would wager on Gore. He came out here for the ride, the rush, and the sense of power and to have a little fun.

The day before the action starts, before Bradley's arrival and the big events begin, there is a sign war masterminded and mediated by the Iowa Democratic Party, scheduled to occur at the convention center, in connection with the JJ Dinner. The rules were explained to both campaigns weeks ago, before I arrived, in order to give them time for preparation. Starting at six P.M., a maximum of five people from each campaign will be given an opportunity to hang signs on a certain wall directly outside the convention room for a period of one-half hour. I don't see it at first. I don't see that a certain twisted someone somewhere is turning us into animals.

For a good portion of the day, volunteers stick thick two-sided poster board tape to small rectangular Bill Bradley signs. By five P.M., we have hundreds of signs stacked and ready for deployment. Mullen, usually reluctant to involve himself in such mundane matters, resolves on accompanying the four other designees down to the convention center. We arrive at five-thirty P.M. with plenty of time to set up, feeling pleased when we locate a ladder for getting to those high, out-of-reach places. It is five minutes to six, and we begin to wonder where the Gore people are, a little giddy at the thought that maybe they have forgotten.

Two minutes later, armies of people like ants march up the stairs and escalators with Gore signs, all sorts of Gore signs, tall ones and small ones, fat ones and long ones. They bring ladders and poles, posters and placards, rope and string, tape and glue. They are ready.

"Let the games begin," announces Rob Tully, the state chair of the IDP. A mass of bodies rush to the wall, jumping over one another, crawling between legs, running this way and that, scrambling to hang signs.

We are far, far outnumbered by the Gore people, and someone from our group cries out, still desperately trying to hang signs, "Hey, whatever happened to the five-person limit?"

The man from the IDP, the state chair with the thin graying hair and the pointed nose, confirms that only five people are allowed to place signs on the wall but then explains that there is no limit to other types of participation. He stands proudly and stiffly at a comfortable distance with his hands clasped tightly behind his back like a severe schoolmaster. From this pose, he declares in the most authoritative voice he can muster that "the Bradley team" is using a forbidden type of tape, one that will damage the walls. Shrieks of objection fly. Some of us hurriedly try to throw masking tape over the forbidden tape, while others, myself included, ignore the schoolmaster's decree, hoping not to have our knuckles rapped.

Gore volunteers and staff continue to march up the stairs and escalators, now with enormous banners attached to tall plastic pipes that have buckets of sand at the base to support them. They can place these signs anywhere; they no longer need walls. Again, our little platoon raises objections, but the man from the IDP, happy to intercede, indicates that since the issue was never specifically discussed, he can see no reason not to widen the playing field. The Gore contingent has already moved toward other walls, toward ceilings, windows, and cracks, until finally the whole building is afloat with the name Gore.

I fall away, stop pulling down their signs and putting ours up, stop fighting for space and ladders and speed. As I drop to the floor, leaning back on my arms, sweat drips off my brow and down my back. Almost through a haze, as though I am at the far end of a long, empty road, I hear people exchanging nasty remarks. I don't know what to think. I don't know if this, like making props of veterans, is typical, or if the IDP and their gray-headed chair have constructed an aberrant ritual worthy of *Lord of the Flies*.

The building is beyond recognition, very much like a great deep blue sky patterned by the gods not with the name Zeus but with the word *Gore*. Looking about me, I feel slight motion sickness, as though I am on a boat or in a car. If this was a battle, we lost bitterly.

The next day, Mullen directs me to buy the chum, or so he dubs it. The word suggests something illicit. I hear it and visualize oily bait scattered across water to lure fish. But the chum that I deal with designates little more than small gifts, tokens of appreciation, such as signed basketballs and autographed copies of Bradley's books, bought for supporters who have given time and energy to the campaign. Chum seems to be the equivalent of a thank-you note sent to an aunt after a long weekend visit to her house in the country, the equivalent of bringing beer to a friend's Super Bowl party.

When the weekend finally begins, when the man himself actually arrives, the trunk of my car is full of chum. Bradley's first event of this particular trip to Iowa, my first event of the campaign, is on Friday, October 8, 1999. It is an afternoon meeting with a group of community college presidents at a hotel in the suburbs of Des Moines. Community colleges are one of Iowa's great success stories, and Bradley will speak before their chiefs, pay homage, and let them take his measure.

After we have set up the sound system and hung the banner and while we are still waiting for Bradley's plane to land, Gabe methodically ties loose ends. He checks the height of the banner. Bradley is tall, and the base of it should be level with his shoulders, lined up just so for the cameras. He tests the fishing wire to make sure the banner is fastened securely. He makes certain that the electrical cords are properly taped to the floor, out of harm's way. He places a glass of water, no ice, never any ice, on the table where Bradley will speak. He conducts a fifth and final sound check to eliminate lingering feedback and static. He runs upstairs to

Bradley's holding room and turns on the air-conditioning. He looks at his watch again and again.

While we wait, I buy a bag of pretzels, hardly enough to answer my hunger pains. Gabe tells me, trying to both go easy and be strong, that we are not really supposed to eat while we are advancing events. I look around me into the carpeted burgundy lobby and, seeing no one, want to tell Gabe he can't be so literal, that this rule, that lots of these rules, has its distinct place and purpose. The eating rule, I want to say, should be applied to the loud and visible munching of popcorn while Bradley is speaking. It should be applied to stuffing a sandwich down your throat as you lead Bradley to the stage. It should not be applied to standing alone in a deserted hotel lobby waiting for a candidate who is still half an hour away.

Gabe's comment reminds me of a memo he and I recently received from the national advance director, which said, among other things, "No excessive smiling at the candidate!" I tried to see the sense in it, guessing that people annoy and distract Bradley with their eager pleasure, but the line infuriated me, and once again, then as now, I clamped down on my tongue, practicing what is for me a little practiced art.

When Bradley's large white van, the one we rented, pulls up, I realize I don't know how to behave. I met him once, the day of my sister's wedding, now nearly ten years ago. I wonder if he is aware that I am out here in Iowa. I would like to make a connection, establish a tie, but I don't wish to court favor or be disagreeably forward.

He is a tall man with a loping gait and, after stopping to hear a few words from Gabe, walks directly to the room of college presidents, who are seated, ready to applaud. I keep at a distance, watching and listening as he moves around the table, shaking hands, learning names, exchanging a line or two. He is slow and deliberate.

After being introduced, he speaks for about fifteen minutes, addressing issues relevant to his audience and delivering a stump speech I will hear again and again. He talks about how politicians should speak more often from their core convictions and not from polls or focus groups. He talks about creating a new politics in America, a politics that's not polluted by money. Campaign finance reform is a priority for Bradley, and he is calling not only for a ban on soft money, but also for publicly financed elections. Furthermore, he believes that at this time of extraordinary prosperity there shouldn't be forty-four million people without health insurance or fourteen million children living in poverty. He outlines his proposals for dealing with these problems. And he mentions (as he will mention in every speech I ever hear him deliver) his determination to heal the racial divide. He is sincere and, unexpectedly, he is funny, so that for a moment I forget how odious my first few days have been.

The next day, Saturday, everyone, including Bradley, is occupied with preparations for the JJ Dinner and the concurrent alternative event. It is my task to advance for – meaning cater to – our entertainer. He is a piano player who won a few – I can never remember how many, although I will be told more than once – Grammy Awards and who also played with the Grateful Dead. I am expected to enjoy this low-pressure task of rubbing shoulders with a celebrity but, as with collecting podiums and buying grape soda, feel sorely underutilized.

Mullen directs me to call the entertainer's agent and find out what we need to supply musically, what he likes, what he reads, what his allergies are. The agent laughs when I dutifully ask if the piano player has allergies, not sure why such information would be of value to me. I explain, resenting in that moment both her and Mullen, that it could have an impact on the food I buy. She assures me that he will need no such pampering but does instruct me to provide room temperature Evian water and extra towels.

This is the first I have heard of the entertainer. I certainly have never seen him before and, fearing that I won't recognize him, decide, before heading to the airport, to place a large Bradley pin on my lapel. Long after the entire entourage of passengers from his flight has filed to baggage claim, I am still waiting, eyeing the crowd. Finally, a tall, almost comically lanky man with a touch of vulnerability in his shoulders approaches me, introduces himself, and then, barely pausing to breathe, asks if I failed to recognize him. Don't I know who he is? Aren't I a fan? His tone is almost pleading. At first I think he must be joking, making fun of famous people, but when I realize that he is serious, I smile, hoping to appease him, preferring not to lie.

On the ride to his hotel, he asks how the room is set up and how many people will be attending our alternative event. When he hears that we intend to have six hundred to a thousand people stand at cocktail tables with their food, he voices strong objections. People at cocktail tables talk, he tells me. People at cocktail tables are sociable. People eating dinner are loud. He, a piano player with no band, needs quiet, needs an attentive audience. He doesn't want to have stop playing in the middle of a set and tell everyone to shut up, no, he certainly does not.

Again, I think he must be joking. This is, after all, a political event, not a concert, and he, a Bradley supporter, is here to help, right? But I look at him and see that he is more than serious, slightly angry, nervous even. Feeling a sudden, sincere, and uncomfortable sympathy for this big man with such visible weakness, I assure him that we are flexible, that the room can easily be rearranged, and more important, that the people of Iowa are very excited for his performance. He looks skeptical, but then after being reminded by his assistant of how many Grammy Awards he's won, he relaxes.

Joan Phonboneski, the spelling I guess at, is what he calls me, after a character from *MAD* magazine. Joan Phonboneski and the piano player spend the evening together, him needy and playful in his lanky, vulnerable sort of way, and me glum and reassuring. After playing a first set for the crowd of Bradley supporters, after that same crowd has begun to watch the live televised feed from the JJ Dinner, he decides that he wants to attend the JJ Dinner. I search for and locate two tickets and, moments later, find myself sitting next to the piano player at a round table surrounded by hundreds and hundreds of identical tables in an expansive room at a great distance from the main stage, at least fifty yards.

The piano player and I discuss his first set while a local politician finishes speaking. "Tell me something, why did you guys ask me to play for that ten extra minutes? I mean, did you need to kill time or was the crowd just grooving?" He leans forward to ask the question.

This time, right from the start, I know that he's not joking. "Well, things were running a bit off schedule, but the crowd clearly wanted to hear more."

"Yeah, it was a decent crowd, but did you notice how that bozo introducing me said that I won only one Grammy Award? You'd think he could at least get his facts straight."

Rob Tully, the master of ceremonies at yesterday's sign war and the chair of the IDP, begins introducing Bradley. We hear a list of accomplishments, a touch of biography, a measure of inspiration, and in conclusion: "It is my honor, ladies and gentlemen, and my great pleasure to introduce to you Senator Bill Bradley." There is great cheering and applause, and the room fills with an energy that is entirely new to me, political energy, spicy and powerful energy.

Bradley approaches the microphone, places a pair of spectacles low on his nose, and begins. He tells a funny story. He talks about his hometown. He appeals to Democratic principles: ". . . the party has to reach out, grab people, and convince them we can do big things. . . . We should never acquiesce to the thought that we can't . . . not in America, not today, not as Democrats. The moral imperative for health care shouldn't scare us; it should energize us. The moral imperative for raising children out of poverty shouldn't scare us; it should energize us. We are Democrats: We've done big things before, and we can do big things again."

He refers to Gore rarely and then only respectfully as the vice president. He compares his race with Gore to baseball's home-run race between Mark McGwire and Sammy Sosa. "Each pushed the other to be better and better and better, and an incredible record was set." He suggests that he and Gore should view their own contest in this light, as valuable incentive, as a catalyst for improving their individual platforms and the platform of the Democratic Party.

His delivery is low-key, many would say too low-key, but I am nervous with admiration. Politicians usually make me want to run. I think them liars. I distrust them. Bradley is honest. Bradley actually believes what he says. I look at the rest of the audience, longing for them to feel as I do. Meanwhile, thick men with army-short hair march up and down the aisles pumping blue-and-white GORE 2000 signs.

Gore takes the stage in cowboy boots and an autumnal suit. He pushes aside the podium and speaks to the crowd with the full vigor of his body, emphasizing with a forceful and practiced motion of the arms his every word. His arms are unencumbered, free to thrash and whirl because he has bucked precedent and chosen a small lavalier microphone, which is attached to his shirt, instead of choosing the full-size microphone used by Bradley and those who preceded him. Gore is on the offensive, firmly replacing his "ignore Bradley" approach, the one he used before Bradley began surging in the polls, with an "attack Bill" approach.

"Stay and fight" is his chosen theme, and as soon as it is revealed, a sea of STAY AND FIGHT signs, distributed by Gore staff, rise into the air. Gore asks his supporters to chant the words with him, and more than half the room rallies to his cry as the thick men with army-short hair pump their signs more robustly than ever. Gore suggests that when Bradley retired from the Senate in 1997, he abandoned Democrats. He tells us that on the one hand there is Bradley, who failed to stay and fight, and on the other there is he,

Gore, a leader with the commitment and wherewithal to stick it out for the good of the people. "I never walked away, I decided to stay and fight." His long white fingers are tensed and extended.

As the words *stay and fight* echo and bounce, I remember Bradley's earlier remark "It takes discipline to be positive." Before I took this job, I watched Bradley's insurgent campaign rise and was delighted to hear and read that he had thus far, always the articles said "thus far," resisted the juicy appeal of negativism. Of course, there were those better schooled in practical politics who mocked my delight, calling it naïve. They said Bradley would fall like Dukakis if he failed to fight back. They said positive campaigning is its own kind of political tactic, but I disagreed. Still, one can't help wondering why negative campaigning has such a hold on us. This is an old and tired question, a question whose edges have been worn dull, but I am new to politics and am stunned and bewildered by the ringing of the battle cry "Stay and fight."

I scan the faces in the room, hoping to gauge the response to Gore's barbs, and find, with very few exceptions, that the responses follow predetermined lines of allegiance. Those with Bradley buttons are inattentive, have their ear half-cocked, or are stiff in their seats. Those with Gore buttons are clapping for Gore, and I get the impression that they would clap just the same if he were reading a paragraph out of an instructional book on checkers. No votes are being won tonight.

A man at our table, a Bradley supporter, who pleased the piano player earlier by asking for his autograph, expresses anger with one exceptionally provoking Gore soldier. This soldier has marched up and down our aisle, about-facing at each end, ten or twenty times already, obstructing our view each time with his STAY AND FIGHT sign. We nod in agreement at the Bradley supporter's invective, and the Bradley supporter stands suddenly just as the soldier passes our table and gives him a good, soldierly slap on the back, leaving behind a large Bradley sticker. The soldier flashes a dirty look at our supporter and resumes his march. A din of snickering can be heard as more and more guests take notice, but the oblivious soldier continues marching for a good five minutes before a fellow soldier finally removes the sticker. The piano player and I return to the alternative event as soon as Gore finishes. He has another performance to deliver.

The alternative event is well attended by our supporters but little attended by the media. I keep looking at the two empty tiers of press risers and wondering when they will come. They do come, but only a meandering few, and I can't help thinking that without a significant media presence, our story about bucking the system will be lost. Yet I gladly dismiss these unpleasant reckonings on the grounds that with one piddling event under my belt, I should not presume to judge. Besides, there is well-orchestrated pandemonium to distract me.

Bill Walton, a former NBA star, and Paul Wellstone, a Minnesota senator, the night's two liveliest speakers, beckon from the stage. They bring great energy to the room, enough to ride the crowd through to Bradley's late arrival from the nearby JJ Dinner. Bill Walton's speech is wildly uninhibited both in its devotion to Bradley and in its disdain for Gore. I have never heard anything quite like it and don't know how to react when his language haphazardly crosses the threshold of propriety. Paul Wellstone is a short man with a firebrand preacher's delivery, who raises his fists into the air with enough force to lift his compact body off the floor and who manages to impress upon the audience a deep and vigorous authenticity. The entertainer follows the speakers with a second set on the piano and seems pleased with the reception and more pleased still when Bradley walks into the room. By altering a few lyrics, he transforms the song that he is in the midst of singing into a Bradley fight song, and the crowd roars.

Ernestine Bradley, the senator's wife, approaches me as things are winding down. She is eight years older than Bradley but looks quite young and retains a beauty marked by direct, shapely features. She is also small, thin, and rippling with energy.

"You are Joan, yes, yes, very nice to see you." She has a German accent but enunciates each word very clearly.

"My sisters always have such wonderful things to say about you." I have met her once before, and she seems to remember this, but I stumble awkwardly over my words. "Oh, and they wanted me to pass on their hellos."

On this point she nods and then asks, "Are you liking Iowa?"

Unsure of how to respond to the candidate's wife, I say something approximating the truth. "There is a big difference between New York and Des Moines and, well, it has been difficult. I guess I'm still hoping to adjust."

Ernestine tilts her head, looks me in the eye, and urges patience before being pulled into the crowd. She turns back and smiles. It is comforting to be acknowledged, and I suddenly feel content. In fact, when the piano player and Bill Walton, who turn out to be old friends, ask me to take them to a bar where they can drink together, it strikes me as an amusing adventure rather than a tedious chore.

Moments later, I hold open a door for Bill Walton as he, a seven-foot man with red hair, pushes through a throng of fans, distributing a stack of his own photographs as he goes. He climbs into my midsize sedan. It is a funny sight. He has to sit in the far back so he can stretch out his legs across the seats, but still his knees collide with the ceiling, and lack of space forces his arm out of the window. He also has difficulty making room for his enormous head, which fits only if held horizontally. The piano player, also tall, pulls the front seat forward to make space for Bill Walton and ends up in almost as preposterous a position. Bill Walton doesn't smell of alcohol but is filled with such hot abandon that I suspect he must be drunk. As I pull out of the garage, he begins a story and tells it with as much animation as the tight quarters allow.

At the start of the JJ Dinner, Bill Walton stood at Bill Bradley's table, and the two men, old basketball buddies, chatted. Bill Walton soon observed Al Gore in the distance, making his way through the crowd. Bill Walton quickly grabbed a pen and paper from his pocket and jotted down a few words. He then folded the paper neatly in his hand, said good-bye to Bradley, and made his way back toward his own table, which took him in the direction of Gore. As Bill Walton got nearer, Gore made a point of disengaging himself from a conversation in order to shake Bill Walton's hand. Gore offered a few pleasant remarks, and Bill Walton gave Gore the folded piece of paper, which Gore opened and read. It said: "Dear Al, I want to thank you in advance for your early withdrawal from the 2000 presidential race. Go, Bradley, go!!" Gore looked up at

Bill Walton, back down at the paper, shook his head, and walked away.

By the end of the story, our whole car is shaking under the force and weight of Bill Walton's laughter. I join in the laughter, but the piano player first wants to know if the story is true. Bill Walton catches his breath, which requires considerable effort, for long enough to assure the piano player that it couldn't be truer and resumes his laughter. All three of us then laugh together. I am not sure what to make of the story, odd and embarrassing as it is, but I am glad to laugh and, in spite of myself, pleased with the company.

I go to bed feeling as if I have entered a new country with unknown moral perils but also fresh promise. Al Gore and Bill Bradley, two of the nation's most prominent politicians, stood onstage in that expansive shell of a conference room and offered a choice of leaders, and with each passing word I found myself more deeply committed to Bill Bradley. Usually there is a miserable contrast between distant veneration of a heroic figure and up-close actuality, but I feel certain as I drift off to sleep that this will never apply to my relationship with Bill Bradley.

The next day, Sunday, October 10, 1999, is full of light. I buy the paper before my early meeting with Gabe. In reference to the JJ Dinner, *The New York Times* says, "Mr. Bradley . . . portrayed himself as the candidate on the high road." The word *portrayed* strikes me as foolishly neutral, and I brush by it, but it is used more than once. I have been reading coverage more closely since I arrived, and the attitude strikes me as typical. It is as if the media can't get around to considering the truth or, alternatively, are too jaded to believe that a high road exists. Either way, it is bunk.

At the JJ dinner, Bradley made a genuine effort to keep things positive. It was evident in his opening words: "Vice President Al Gore, it's a pleasure to be with you for the first time on the same platform and I welcome other times." Good-bye to cross-firing denunciations; that is what I heard. I heard an uncompromising challenge to the course of American politics. Bradley and Gore were poles apart.

Gore was free with his use of the name Bill. "I listened carefully, Bill, to what you had to say about making this campaign a different kind of experience and lifting up our democracy. I really agree with that, I think we have a chance to do exactly that. But you know the best way to do that is to have regular debates on the issues. Let's have one every week. What about it? Let's have a debate on agriculture in Iowa right now. What about it, Bill? If the answer is yes, stand up and wave your hand." The "stand up and wave your hand" bit was insulting and hollow, but the repeated and sarcastic use of Bradley's first name really put me over the edge. *The New York Times* frames it, all of it, however, as Gore's invigorated attempt to reenergize his campaign. I take a few jabs at the open air and jump into my rented white Pontiac.

My earlier dilemma about how to address Bradley, about names and titles, suddenly seems childish. When my parents asked to be called Dan and Pryde, I thought of names as a great equalizer. I did not see that names are also weapons. Gore used "Bill" like a fist, to take shots at Bradley. He used it to shatter any sense of formal and respectful distance, to disparage and condescend. He showed me that names level and lift, flatten and bloat, protect and molest. Ironically, he firmed my resolve to address Bradley as "Senator."

The Dunn family farm is on the outskirts of Des Moines, and the day is so bright that I consider wearing my sunglasses, until it occurs to me that sunglasses, dark and forbidding as they can appear, might be "off message." The phrase *off message* is new to me and the concept even newer, but I have heard it more than once in the past few days and have absorbed much of its meaning. Sunglasses pose the off-, on-message question and its inherent dilemmas rather comically. There is the message, and then there is conviction. Of course, you hope that the two cohere, that conviction and message come together to mount a strong front, but when the two diverge, you must choose. Does the pale woman from New York with the short dark hair and the slim black suit make herself accessible to a tranquil group of struggling Iowa farmers by keeping the sunglasses in her pocket, or does the lonely girl who is squinting from the glare put on sunglasses to protect her eyes and to make herself more comfortable as she sets up rows of chairs on the grass? I leave the sunglasses in my pocket and resolve to get Gabe's opinion at the first opportunity.

Gabe is light on his feet, apparently relieved to be through with preparations for the JJ Dinner. He is pleased, too, I think, that there were no major slipups, at least none on the advance end. The only slipup I have heard mentioned relates to the American flags we distributed at the beginning of the alternative event. Mullen wanted flags as added flavor, but the ones we bought were made in China, and good union-minded Democrats buy items made in America. A member of the press noticed the oversight and pointed to it, but fortunately the incident ended there. There were no offended guests or damaging articles.

In front of the chairs is a microphone, and behind the microphone is a long, narrow hog run, now empty and intended as a weighty testament to the plight of the Iowa farmer. Beyond the hog run are endless fields of corn, truly golden in the sun, on land that is not quite flat. Next to the microphone is a podium, like the one I searched for in hotels, attics, and warehouses, but we ended up using one of the very first podiums we looked at, one from the orange warehouse, one Gabe took me to see right after my arrival. It looks just fine, certainly much better than any of the others would have looked. Opposite the podium, to the rear of the chairs and press risers, is the Dunn house, fronted by a small red porch. On the porch are ham-and-cheese sandwiches and crisp red apples and pitchers of sweet, sweet lemonade. In between the house and the chairs is a small homemade basketball hoop, entertainment for two wholesome boys, who have just chased their basketball into the barn.

I know by now to set out far fewer chairs than are actually needed. If you have 80 confirmed attendees and 120 expected attendees, then you set out 50 chairs. There is nothing worse than shots of a candidate standing opposite empty chairs and certainly no harm in adding chairs at the last minute for effect, in front of an attentive press corps. We are selling a product, and this is advertising, or so it would seem. Mullen says that impression is everything. However, impression is delicate. When a guy named Bobby suggests that we put hay bales behind the podium, Bobby is told by Gabe and Mullen that hay bales are "Gore-ish," meaning too Hollywood, too produced. Yet Gabe and Mullen have just asked Joe Dunn to move his tractor, an enormous brand-new green tractor, up for a cutaway shot.

This is sales, and it appears that people respond to the image, not to substance, that the public doesn't want reality, but rather well-crafted visions of greatness, of great men and great moments, tempered by touches of humanity, like the sad and empty hog run. The only practical problem, forget the moral ones, with this approach is that Bradley hates to be handled. If you tell him to jump in the air, then he takes a defiant seat. This, Mullen instructs, will be the great challenge for us, "a talented but inexperienced crew."

Bradley is running a little late, which wouldn't be a problem if all the guests weren't squinting uncomfortably beneath the high, hard sun. One particularly old woman in a wheelchair is desperate for a hat and is very sorry that she didn't bring one. I play with the idea of lending her my sunglasses, still in my pocket, and smile at the thought of them on her handsome but worn face. Instead we give her a cap borrowed from the Dunn house, and at long last, a cloud of dust lifts above the quiet dirt road. The crowd takes it as a sign of Bradley's imminent arrival. The cloud swirls, lengthens, and billows over the corn in the clear blue sky. It is an extraordinary sight, especially since the cars beneath are not yet visible. I feel happy, and as the dark cloud nears, we see that a long line of press vans trails Bradley's vehicle, which heightens still more the suspense and drama. The press scrambles out of the vehicles while Gabe leads Bradley into the Dunn house. Bradley ducks beneath the door frame as he enters.

When he reemerges, Mullen is frothing at the bit. Mullen is dead set on getting Bradley to play basketball with the two boys at the homemade hoop, and the press, thinking along the same lines, has prepared its cameras for the shot. Gabe whispers something to Bradley, perhaps making the suggestion directly, and leads him toward the hoop. Who knows what Bradley would have done if he were more of an actor, if he were not feeling pushed, if the little boys were not in harm of becoming props? Bradley smiles at the boys, raises his eyebrows as one of their shots drops through the hoop, and walks right on by. Mullen is furious.

We didn't get the shot of Bradley on the farm at the homemade hoop with the two wholesome boys, but the man introducing Bradley starts things off on just the right note. This man says he has always known that Bradley was a straight-thinking individual, but that he was especially amused and impressed just a moment ago. The man then launches into a story: "Did you-all see the senator go into the Dunn house? Well, while he was in that house he used the bathroom, and after he used the bathroom, he asked to borrow some tape. 'What kind of tape?' we asked right back. You see, the senator had quite a few of folks in that house with him. 'Scotch tape will do,' the senator told us. The senator then took that tape with him into the bathroom, made use of it, and returned it. Well, I was curious, and as we walked over here, I asked the senator why he had wanted that tape. The senator gave me a sly look and flipped over his tie, which was slightly torn but being held together by nothing other than a piece of Scotch tape."

Everyone has a good laugh, and the introducer reaches over to Bradley, smiles up at him, turns over his tie, and displays the taped underside for everyone to see. A loose strand of Bradley's hair, tossed straight up into the air by the wind, makes it all seem real.

At the end of the day, after Bradley has left Iowa to campaign in other states, I phone my sister Jenny. "Damn it, Joan, why haven't you called? Have I sent you to hell? I saw Bradley on television last night at an Iowa fund-raiser and I looked for you. Were you there? Wasn't he wonderful? Tell me everything."

3

Mad-Dash Existence

I would rather be right than be president.
—Henry Clay

"SLAUGHTER RATES RUNNING above expectation . . . Wheat one-half to one-quarter cent lower . . . Decline in corn and soybean yield . . . Weekend rainfall in Brazil causing flux in the price of . . ." These radio announcements, arriving routinely like New York traffic reports, alter my frame of mind. They give edge, new dimension, to surroundings that otherwise strike me as dull and altogether too American. They send me firm notice that Iowa, despite the monotony of white faces and fried food, despite the glut of chain stores and chain restaurants, is a place very different from any I have known. Iowa is a solid entity existing on its own terms, where farmers, who raise hogs and cultivate corn, are bound oddly and inextricably to national and international markets, to rising slaughter rates and weekend rainfall in Brazil. Iowa is as strip-mall ordinary and as Grand Canyon unique as any state in the country. Its cornfields and hog runs are as all-American and as singular as the cowboys of Texas and the skyscrapers of New York.

The Thoreau Center is not yet in view, but I know that after the road dips, it will be visible at the top of the hill. The dip is now familiar to me. Last night, I traced and retraced the route from Bradley's hotel to the center in order to complete driving directions, noting exact mileage at every bump and turn. Driving directions, an advance responsibility, facilitate the candidate's timely arrival, and as I, in my newness, clumsily endeavored to make them perfect, I found that this particular dip, each time I crossed it, reminded me of my father. When I was a little girl, my father would press down on the accelerator at the approach of a dramatic rise or a sudden fall in the road, which created the effect of a roller coaster as we soared along. He scrunched his eyes and I tensed my stomach and together at the moment of impact we yelled, "Alleeooop!"

It is early on October 16. I am en route to my first solo event, which by chance, or maybe not, is a gay event. I have prepared at length, for it has been made exceedingly clear to me that a single mistake can have enormous repercussions. Every detail matters – that is what I am told, that is the credo of the advance person. And while I am somewhat resistant to this mentality, to being held accountable for where Bradley goes to the bathroom and for how his tie looks, I do not ever want to do him or his campaign harm; so with earnest resolve, I have, over the course of the past few days, gone through my checklist of responsibilities.

I sketched the location, identifying all possible entrances and exits and all power sources. I learned how to pronounce the names of relevant individuals and towns. I found convenient parking and looked for the "union bug," the surest indication that an item is union-made, on banners and placards. I distinguished east from west so I could prevent the rising sun from intruding on the press shot. I searched for lawn mowers, playgrounds, anything that might create distracting sounds in the middle of the speech. I secured a holding room, equipped with phone and fax. I counted chairs. I said thank you often, knowing that it is my job to please political leaders and members of the community. I tried to anticipate everything that could go wrong. In short, I did exactly what I had been taught.

Today, the day of the event, there are other considerations. Keep out of the picture. Stay five to ten yards in front of Bradley. Maintain eye contact. Make sure the room is not half-empty. Avoid speaking to the press about anything other than the weather. Do not allow bright lights to shine in Bradley's face. Use American-made products. Remain composed. Tell the truth. Obey the law. Have Bradley's vehicle and driver waiting for him sufficiently in advance of his departure at a designated site. The idea is that proper advance work enables the candidate to focus on communicating his message effectively. The idea is that the advance person assists the press in reporting favorably on the campaign.

As I pull up to the building, which is distinguished by an attractive brick façade and large elegant windows, the host, a politically active gay man, waves to me from the lawn. He is the owner and founder of the Thoreau Center. We walk inside together. On a table near the entrance, there are cold carrots and celery. Coffee is in an adjacent room next to a toppling stack of foam cups. A man in a purple suit is already seated. I stare for several seconds at the man's shoes, also purple, before understanding my own surprise, revelation. Life not only exists between New York and Los Angeles, but it also exists in a variety of shades. One of those shades sits before me in a purple suit waiting to hear Bradley speak. He, like rainfall in Brazil and rising slaughter rates, gives unforeseen breadth to Iowa.

The event is still two hours away, but I am told it will take every bit of two hours, even for a small event like this – there will not be more than fifty people – to put things in place. Arranging chairs, hanging banners, and setting up a sound system take time. I talk with the host. He is ready to introduce Bradley. He knows that Bradley plans to take questions. He knows that I will signal him when it is time for Bradley to leave and that he will then have to bring a subtle end to the questions so that Bradley does not have to cut anyone off and so that Bradley has an opportunity to shake hands. I place a glass of water without ice on a table next to the microphone and tape sound cords to the floor. I try to make sure that nothing has been overlooked.

Fifteen minutes before Bradley's scheduled arrival, I stand outside and wait. The sound system is not working perfectly. There is feedback, which, as far as I can tell, can be avoided only if the volume is kept low. I will have to tell Bradley, who is soft-spoken, to keep the microphone close to his mouth.

The thought of telling him, a man notoriously resistant to being handled, to do anything, racks my nerves. It also brings a sense of excitement that seems, unaccountably, to be emanating from a certain spot beneath my kneecaps. I feel like a child in costume, like a child in an older brother's baseball uniform or in a mother's dress. The excitement and the chill October wind, my suit, and my cell phone benignly conspire to put me in "advance" character, and it feels fine.

I have entered another universe, as people periodically do, where the epicenter of movement, the marrow of thought, is altogether different. There are a multitude of universes to enter, to happen upon: The computer programmer peeks into the dog show; the fan goes backstage; the bohemian playwright moves to Hollywood. Each time you walk into a hair salon or a bike shop or a locker room, the world begins rotating on a different axis. I am in a universe where Iowa has met politics, and right now, the air and the sunshine seem perfectly aligned.

Bradley arrives on schedule. He lowers his head to get out of the vehicle, as big men must often do, and pauses to adjust his overcoat.

"Senator" – without thinking this is how I address him – "you will have to hold the microphone close to your mouth because of a problem we're having with the sound." I wait with some trepidation for a reaction. It is hard to know how he, a career politician, will respond to directives from me, a greener-than-green hireling.

Without a thought, with plain good humor, he says, "I am putty in your hands, Joan." I bow my head. My face is red with pleasure and amusement. The thought of straightening his tie no longer bothers me. I lead him inside.

Bradley has always struck me as a conservative man. He was the only son of conservative churchgoing parents in conservative churchgoing Crystal City, Missouri. He has forever been a square, a Goody Two-shoes, the Mississippi River's antidote to Tom Sawyer and Huckleberry Finn – Bradley too was raised on the banks of the Mississippi. But a highly developed sense of responsibility, of fairness and justice, makes him a liberal politician. Ever since learning of this event, I have wondered how he, a personally conservative, politically liberal man, will behave when confronted by a gay and lesbian audience, by a room of purple suits and tall, busty blondes with protruding Adam's apples.

He lopes in and shakes hands. He does not modify his behavior one speck. There is not a single false or affected gesture. He is entirely himself: a stiff, wise square with an inclusive heart and mind. This impresses me, but I am impressed most of all with his straightforward responses to difficult questions.

"Do you believe in gay marriage?"

"No." He does not sidestep the bad news, as politicians so frequently do. He does not deflect. He does not offer up sugar-coated particulars, hoping his audience will forget that he never answered the question. He says no. He answers directly and honestly, and this, in the world of politics, is its own sort of miracle. Then he provides a more complete account of his views. He supports granting gays and lesbians all the benefits and privileges of married heterosexual couples, but he does not support gay marriage. He thinks that there is too much potential for offending the religious sensibilities of too large a portion of the population.

I already knew this. Flo says that no mainstream politician of high ambition supports gay marriage, that it simply is not a politically viable position. Of course, I think that any adult couple who pleases should be able to marry, but this is not an issue of great importance to me. It is important to members of the audience, though, and I want them to like Bradley. I want them to know that he expresses his deepest convictions when he says, "We're a good people." He believes, "There's goodness in most of us." He says to every audience, no matter what the composition, "And whenever I see somebody who can see beneath skin color or eye shape or sexual orientation to the individual, I think to myself All of us could be that good."

Bradley's stump speech, a fixed composite of stories and proposals, is becoming familiar to me. I can already finish some of his sentences. Still, I listen attentively from the back of the room because there are always slight variations in the sequence and tone and because he often adds detail about topics that are of particular interest to the audience in front of him. As I listen, I also pray, not directed, deliberate prayers, but tensed, physical prayers. I badly want the campaign to succeed.

In the midst of my prayers, Gabe calls. Teresa, the third advance person here in Iowa, one of seven nationwide, had a car accident after running a red light. She is safe but unavailable. I have been left with her responsibilities. I have wanted more responsibility. I have wanted it the way a kid in a classroom, hand raised, body bouncing out of the chair, wants to be called on.

As soon as this event is over, I will have to dash to the 4-H Bingley Building at Marion County Fairground in Knoxville, Iowa. Bradley has only one event between this one at the Thoreau Center and the one at the fairground. I will not have much time. Allison, my roommate, the local field organizer, will be waiting for me. I should pick up an American flag on the way. The flag they planned on using for a backdrop is stuck in the trunk of Teresa's totaled car.

Gabe tells me that it is essential in this particular setting to follow flag etiquette. I ask him to elaborate. He runs through what he calls the basics and then suggests that I consult the flag etiquette memo I received. He warns that the American flag is nothing to trifle with in Knoxville, Iowa. I latch on to his sense of urgency with unexpected satisfaction.

Meanwhile, Bradley, who is still taking questions, decides to sit on the table where I placed his glass of water. The table's leg begins slowly, almost imperceptibly at first, to fold inward, threatening to collapse and bring Bradley down with it. The checklist says make sure all tables and podiums are stable; it is just the sort of cautious admonition that has curled my lip, made me jeer. Now, somewhere, an impish spirit is laughing at me.

Another staff member notices the folding leg and whispers in alarm that we will all be fired if Bradley ends up on the floor amid fragments of a broken table with these two news cameras at our heels ready to pounce. I stand in pained and frozen anticipation. The thought of cutting Bradley off in midsentence, of inserting myself into the discussion with such unfortunate tidings to the possible alarm and irritation of him and everyone else, is more than I can, at this introductory phase of my advance career, fathom.

Luckily, it occurs to me to that Matt Henshon, Bradley's "body person," his number one assistant, his shadow of many months, will have more pluck, and in fact, as soon as I inform Matt, he interrupts Bradley, who is in the midst of answering a question, to point out with well-crafted directness the danger posed by the folding leg. Bradley looks down at the leg, which is now slanting deeply. He then assures Matt and his audience, without moving a solitary inch, with an amused but also willful smile, that he will catch himself and the water should the table break.

After the event, I rush ahead to Marion County Fairground in Knoxville, stopping along the way to buy an American flag. Allison is obviously alarmed by the unexpected turn of events and generously hopeful that I, though new, prove capable. She is also without a car, which probably doubles her anxiety. She left her car behind, anticipating that an advance person would be present much earlier, and got a ride here. Her car is foreign. She could not risk causing offense to our supporters, hardworking men and women who believe, heart and soul, in Americans buying American products.

Crowd building for Bradley in this area, union territory, where support for Gore is strong, is already hard enough. At this event, we expect no more than fifteen to twenty people. Still, fifteen to twenty people are nothing to overlook in Iowa's world of living room politics. In fact, for this precinct caucus – a precinct is a subdivision of a county – probably fewer than fifteen people will show up to vote.

Campaigning in Iowa and New Hampshire, in the words of George Stephanopoulous, is intimate. It is the most intimate part of presidential primaries. Candidates are forced to meet people in their homes and on the factory floor. They are forced to talk to them over cupcakes and ham sandwiches in barns and church basements on weekdays and Saturday afternoons. Only in Iowa and New Hampshire do candidates still go door to door. As Hunter S. Thompson wrote in *Fear and Loathing: On the Campaign Trail '72:* "There is no Secret Service . . . no vast and everpresent staff of hired minions and police escorts . . . the candidates drive around . . . in rented Fords accompanied by only a handful of local workers and press people and they actually walk into living rooms and try to explain themselves – taking any and all questions face to face . . ."

After Iowa and New Hampshire, everything is different, or so I am told. The events get bigger, the costs higher, and the shielding of candidates more intense. After Iowa and New Hampshire, there is far more media campaigning, which allows the candidate and the candidate's environment to be controlled. Up-close and unscreened encounters with the public become, to some extent, a thing of the past.

Allison and I rush to get the room in order. I hang the flag, making sure that nothing is above or to the right of it; making sure that the stars are, when you look at it, in the upper-left-hand corner; and making sure that it stays well above the ground. Allison prepares name tags and puts out campaign literature. The room is small with low ceilings in a deserted recess of the fairground beside the closed gates of a stadium. In the summer, the stadium is probably home to animal shows, stock car races, and the occasional circus. Boarded-up food stands encircle it. Beyond, a large empty parking lot stretches like an extended limb toward the highway lights. Clouds of dirt rise up and fade in the darkening sky. I have stepped outside to make a phone call, to find out if Bradley is running on schedule. The reception is better outside.

I kick a discarded can of Miller Lite. Beneath it lies a glove. The glove is daintier than what one would expect to find here. I stare at it for a while, trying to imagine the person who dropped it. Then, just as I bend to pick it up, an old woman wanders out of the dusk.

She wears a long brown skirt and the sort of soft, flat sneakers that old women often put on their tender, swollen feet. I half expect to see in her hand the matching glove. She has not come for the glove, though. She is curious about the light that has seeped into the night through the building's open door.

Without saying a word, she walks past me and peers into the room where Allison is still setting up. At first, Allison does not notice her. She pauses to read the Bill Bradley placards and then, startling both of us, says, "I saw him on television. He is the tall feller, ain't he?" Her voice is altogether at odds with her appearance; it is dainty like the glove. I am tongue-tied, but Allison has the presence of mind to invite the woman to our event. Allison even names the people expected to attend, assuming perhaps that the woman will recognize the names and be encouraged. The woman respectfully declines and wanders back into the night.

Everything goes well. Allison leaves with Bradley. She, a field person who has been in this state for months and who is well informed about local politics, needs time to brief him about the day's two remaining events. I pack up alone and, feeling hungry and tired, skip ahead to the Jasper County Democrats chili supper, where Nancy Parrot is scheduled to introduce Bill Bradley to a large and hostile union crowd. Gabe has asked for my help.

The setting is remote. There are not many towns. I follow one main road. The roads that cross it are few and far between, but they are numbered, as roads are sometimes numbered in big cities. The numbers fly up and up. First, I see 21st Street, when I never saw 1st Street, and then, the next thing I see, aside from the cornstalks, is 95th Street. Then 123rd Street is followed by 223rd Street, and up it goes. Perhaps Iowa and all of its little towns once expected or still expect to grow suddenly and magnificently. It is as though they want to leave open the possibility of becoming Chicago or Detroit.

Gore supporters, union men, are picketing outside, holding GORE 2000 signs, holding STAY AND FIGHT signs in their cold, pink hands. Bradley arrives only a few minutes after I do. The intervening event, the one between Knoxville and here, must have been brief. He jumps out of his vehicle, almost before it stops, to shake the cold, pink hands of these picketers. The wind has become bitter. The picketers hardly know how to respond to his sporting advances. Hesitantly they drop their signs and put their hands into his. Most cannot help smiling. A few accompany him inside.

I hold open the door as he walks past, suddenly feeling small and pointless, the way I did when I first arrived in Iowa. It makes things worse when I discover that my help is needed not now, but after the event is over. Gabe has to go to the airport and would like me to break down the sound system. First, though, Bradley will speak. Then, after Bradley speaks and departs, after dinner is eaten, the event organizers will hold an auction. It will be eleven or midnight before I get home.

Dan Lucas, the state director, Pete D'Allessandro, the field director, and Matt Henshon, the body man, stand at the back of the room in amused unity. I stand alone. I am new. My only connection here is to Bradley, and this is a generalized, impersonal connection characterized by mindless servitude and distant adoration. I watch Gabe lead him to the stage. I consider grabbing a bowl of Jasper County chili but remember that Gabe, vigorously attentive to his responsibilities, would disapprove.

As the night wears on, I find myself, not allowed to eat and with no higher purpose than winding sounds cords, resenting Bradley for his importance and everyone else for underestimating my own. I suppose you do not have to be a candidate to be in love with your own potential. Anyway, it is a lesson in humility, in being in the shadow.

During the speech, I isolate myself, out of pride, egotistically disliking every moment of it for not making me more central to it. Growing up as the youngest in a family of ten, always surrounded by an atmosphere of love and adoration, where hard words and looks were, in some ways, unknown, I feel suddenly like the discarded glove. Maybe playing a drudge of a rather low order, whose business is to serve sources of power, will be good for me. Maybe it will be the maturing experience that my mother predicted. My mother thinks it will give me humility, which is what my father said when my knee exploded. It is a funny thing, both of my parents talking so often about humility with me.

In my first two weeks of college, at fall lacrosse practice, I tore three of four ligaments in my right knee, shredded cartilage, dislocated my kneecap, and broke off a piece of my femur. All my life, I had been an athlete. All my life, I had dreamed of defying precedent, of making the female debut in professional soccer, basketball, football, it did not matter. I was recruited to play college lacrosse. Then this happened to my knee, and I felt bereft, like a drummer without a hand, like a singer without a voice. I spent the first several months of college on crutches. I sat on the sidelines for an entire season. I worked three hours every day for a year on rehabilitation.

My father, who wrote me letters throughout college, or rather until he got sick, told me that it would give me humility. He thought I was brazen, that I took too many risks. He hoped that I would stop scoffing at life's dangers. Toward the end of the year, when my knee was closer to healed, he wrote me a letter that I recently found tucked away in a book that he gave me.

Darling Daughter —

Want to tell you in writing how proud I am of you this year — the leg was a horror for you — and you carried it off beautifully — sorry you had to face something like that so soon at Yale, but you probably would agree that it gave you a new view on life — perhaps not as mind-boggling as the physicists' newest and greatest discovery of the beginning of the cosmos — have you read the paper recently? One physicist said it is like looking — almost — into the eye of God — They have pinpointed the beginning of Time/Space — Creation — 15 billion years ago — possibly, incredibly the whole universe came out of a "white" pea-sized something that exploded — Religion and Science now have a single ground of questioning — the first billionth of a second is still ahead to be found, but it is another thing to examine the billionth of a second before the Bang. Anyway, keep reading the paper.

Will be up to get you soon — can't believe an entire year has gone — it will all pass so quickly for you — have as much fun — and learn a little too — as you can.

See you soon and lots of love, Dad

I do not think I ever responded in writing to his letters.

On my way home from Jasper County, I buy gas at a chain called *Kum & Go*. Every time I pass a *Kum & Go* sign, I look twice. The letters are white. The background is pulsating red. You would think that here, in the heart of the Midwest, where wholesome American families are made, someone would object. The name is better suited to a whorehouse or a pornographic video store than a sprawling gas franchise. It is funny, though. I laugh. I just do not know if anyone is laughing with me. It seems possible that these Iowans in their chipper rectitude have failed to notice.

I am likely to be in Iowa, hopping from *Kum & Go* to chili supper, until January 24, 2000, which is when Iowa's first-in-the-nation caucuses are being held. Every four years, in the summer before the general election, the Republican and Democratic Parties hold national conventions for, among other things, the purpose of nominating their party's presidential candidate. In order to win either of these two nominations, a candidate must collect pledges from a majority of his, or perhaps someday her, party's delegates. The delegates are elected from within the states. The two main methods used, at present, to allocate delegates to presidential candidates are the caucus, which is a party meeting, and the primary, which is a ballot-driven election. The caucus is the older method, the one that was used when political parties were born; but in the constantly evolving process of nominating candidates, it has been replaced, in large part, by the primary. In fact, Iowa is one of only a small number of states that still use the caucus, and Iowa is the first state to begin selecting delegates.

In the mid-1980s, Iowa's political leaders cut a deal with New

Hampshire's political leaders: Iowa got the first caucuses, which it basically had had since 1972, and New Hampshire got the first primary. For many years, the arrangement worked. No feuds were triggered: Iowa did not change its caucuses to a primary, and New Hampshire held steady in second. A few days ago, however, New Hampshire unexpectedly scheduled its primary for February 1 and refused to push back the date despite Iowa's entreaties. It had been thought that Iowa would hold its caucuses on January 31 and that New Hampshire would hold its primary on February 8.

Iowa was not happy. The new arrangement threatened to dilute its impact on the presidential selection process. Being the definitive first has all sorts of benefits. Candidates and campaigns flock to Iowa, war chests in hand, poised to pump life into the economy. The media then arrive, and Iowa, a sparsely populated farm state, swiftly becomes the focus of national attention. As the first stop in the race for the presidency, Iowa gets to provide the initial test for presidential candidates, which puts it, a state with only seven electoral votes, in a uniquely powerful position. Iowa did not intend to relinquish all of this to New Hampshire; it was determined to preserve its first-in-the-nation status. It promptly moved its own caucuses up to January 24.

From my perspective, the result is good. I have one less week to spend in Iowa. Still, from now, a cold morning in mid-October, until January 24, my home is here. I try to make it work. I buy a membership to a YMCA in downtown Des Moines. Early in the morning, I play basketball alone in the gym. The time feels stolen. Already, all time away from the campaign feels stolen. Empty gyms, though, are irresistible to me; they have such romance about them.

My fantasies flow onto their vacant floors the way life flows from the sea.

This morning, several mornings after the chili supper, I have promised to make fifty foul shots before heading to the office. It feeds my long-held fantasy of becoming a professional athlete. These are the hard hours of lonely sacrifice that everyone will talk about when I have a gold medal dangling from my neck; or when, a few years down the road, after a decade of playing pickup on public courts, I forge my way into the Women's National Basketball Association.

I have lots of fantasies. In another, Bradley unexpectedly stops by this very gym for a workout of his own. I do not see him at first. He catches my attention by shooting a long, nothing-but-net jumper over my head into the basket. I match his with one of my own. He and I play together. He asks me a few questions. We leave bound by respect and affection.

In reality, the gym is not even empty. There is a big, fat, middle-aged man sitting on the floor with his legs splayed. He palms an undersized basketball and stares contentedly at the floorboards.

I do other things to entertain myself in Des Moines, to make my time here more enjoyable. I visit the Capitol building, the city's centerpiece, in a free moment. I try as many different restaurants as I can. I stop occasionally at stores, ones that sell hunting equipment or religious books, ones of unknown character. I make a project of photographing every bail bonds business I come across.

Before moving to Iowa, I had never seen a bail bonds business. I thought bounty hunters were extinct. I thought that *Midnight Run* was a product of Hollywood nostalgia. Here, though, bail bonds businesses are everywhere. They are like bodegas in New York City or ski shops in Colorado. My favorite is called Jail Busters. *Ghostbusters*, the movie, is clearly their inspiration. On the window, in a red circle with a line through him, there is the cartoonish figure of a man in prison stripes. Next to this, both above and below their phone number, it says, "Who ya gonna call?" Then, in enormous letters, they have painted the words *Jail Busters*.

In this same spirit of immersion and exploration, I went to a gay bar called the Garden. It is one of the only gay bars I have ever visited. I have never felt particularly linked to the gay community. In college, I dated men mostly. The bar was fun. I played pool with two lesbians and their two straight sisters. The crowd was a mix of the old and young, gay and straight, male and female. At around ten o'clock, male dancers, some awkwardly thin, stepped onto a tiny stage in chintzy homemade costumes and stripped down to their fraying thongs while the audience threw dollar bills at them. It was strange. It was entertaining. It was the closest I ever came to seeing a strip show.

We often go to bars. My colleagues go almost every night, but late, after work. They go to sports bars. Most of them would not go to the Garden. I keep returning to a sense of surprise about how conventional and, in some cases, how apolitical they are. Recently, I asked a guy on our staff who does advance work for the press corps and who is about my age why he decided to enter politics. His last job was on Capitol Hill. He looked at me curiously, as if it were an odd question, and said that he had not gone into politics. He does not see himself or his job as particularly political. He sees it in much more concrete terms, in terms of his day-to-day activities, which involve providing logistical services to a group of people that happens to be a campaign press corps. His comments left me feeling lost, as though I had it all backward.

On another occasion, I had a conversation with a young woman on staff whose parents had promised to buy her a car and who intends to make a career in Washington, D.C. She wanted advice on what sort of car to request. Her first choice was a sports utility vehicle, an SUV. I pointed out that SUVs can be hazards to other vehicles and to the environment. She stared at me in silence and then asked, "Are you an environmentalist?" She might just as easily have been asking if I was a Communist or a Moonie, she sounded so alarmed.

It seems that the young people who end up in Washington are not necessarily the young people who occupy themselves in college with ideas of effecting change. In fact, the most issue-oriented, the most politicized, young people on staff are often those who have, like me, come from outside of politics. This sort of observation could lend itself to any number of conclusions, but there is some consensus about the fact that Bradley has attracted more than his fair share of the people who normally shy away from politics, and I think he has done this by offering a sense of hope, a sense that politics can be something more than the dirty art of swallowing lies.

After the chili supper in Jasper County, Andrew Colao, our boss, the national advance director, sent Gabe to Chicago. Jay Carson, the Jay Mullen knows, is here to help me prepare for Bradley's next trip. Jay spends most of his time doing advance work for Bradley in California. He is younger than I am. He just graduated from college but has done advance work before on Charles Schumer's

Senate campaign in New York. He loves the advance lifestyle. He loves Bradley. He loves the pace and the movement. He does not agonize. He is happy to play the game.

In the interest of fun, even though it is less efficient, we travel around Iowa together as we prepare for Bradley's next trip. I have a friend in Iowa City; so does he. Iowa City is a university town about a hundred miles east of Des Moines. It has vegetarian restaurants and trendy bookstores to distinguish it from the rest of Iowa, which is unapologetically out of step. We pay our friends a visit on the way to Davenport.

Davenport has a more traditional look than Iowa City. It sits on the banks of the Mississippi, right across from Illinois. Davenport, Bettendorf, Rock Island, and Moline are known as the Quad Cities. We drive over the Mississippi to Rock Island, Illinois, just to satisfy our caprice. I am delighted to be so near to it, to the great, the magnificent, the majestic Mississippi. For me, the Mississippi, Mark Twain's Mississippi, full of steamboats, thunder, and calamity, is the essence of adventure.

I dreamed of this, not of this particular moment but of this feeling, when I took the job. I have an ice-cream cone and I am looking down into the muddy waters of America's greatest river. Behind me there are rusty railroad tracks, remnants of a bygone era. The sun is shining brightly. I feel broad and alive, like the Mississippi. I thought that I joined the campaign to contribute, to help change things, as part and parcel of my youthful plots to save the world. But it occurs to me that maybe I simply wanted to see life, to visit small, pleasant towns with barges and riverboats.

This is my state of mind when Andrew Colao calls. After

Bradley's upcoming trip to Iowa, Andrew is sending Jay back to California and me home to New York for a brief stint. He needs my help with a fund-raiser at Madison Square Garden. This is the nature of advance work: You wait for you know not who to send you you know not where. I feel blessed to be going home to New York, to Flo, to it all. In the meantime, Jay and I have a trip to plan.

We aim to spend the night in Cedar Rapids. We have done most of what needs to be done in Davenport. We met with deacons at the African American church that Bradley will visit. We found a spot for the town hall meeting. We ate lunch with the local field organizer and a key local politician. We called vendors. Our remaining task is to visit the host of a Davenport fund-raiser that Bradley is scheduled to attend.

The host lives in an ostentatious house, the kind you might see in a New York City suburb but that I did not expect to see in Iowa. He is extremely welcoming. He shows us his wine cellar. He opens a special bottle for us. We drink it happily.

On the way to Cedar Rapids, as Jay points out the world's biggest truck stop, which extends for miles and miles, we make plans to meet Norm, a coworker, a local field organizer, who is from Cedar Rapids. Norm takes us to the best steak restaurant in town, where we eat excessively, drink more excessively, and are altogether merry. After dinner, Norm leads us to a pub. We order Miller Lite, union beer, as advised. We settle in for the night on the floor of Norm's family home on a street lined with trees and nice, well-kept houses that have pumpkins on their doorsteps and neatly raked piles of leaves in their yards.

In the morning, we are going to sort out the details of a meeting

Bradley intends to have with the president of the Cedar Rapids Teamsters local. The AFL-CIO, a league of national and international labor unions, has recently endorsed Gore; but the Teamsters, one of its affiliates, have refused to commit, and the Teamsters, with a national membership of 1.4 million, are worth something, especially in Iowa, where turnout is low and organized labor strong. In Iowa, organized labor makes phone calls, sends letters, produces videos, hires polling firms, and sets up mock caucuses to secure victory for its candidate. In Iowa, organized labor puts union precinct captains at virtually all of the caucus sites, which is, given the fact that there are no secret ballots, almost the same as having a union official inside the voting booth.

The Teamsters hall is in a flat, windowless building on a road that runs parallel to the highway. The buildings in this part of Cedar Rapids are all flat and windowless. This is the no-man's-land that one finds in every city, where warehouses thrive and where people are seldom seen. The landscape is still and colorless, except for a solitary person walking to a solitary vehicle and except for a splash of gold on the Teamsters sign.

I feel slightly hung over. I also feel strange about going inside the building. Jay has a trim beard. I have short hair. Both of us have slim figures and dark clothes. We stand out in downtown Des Moines. Here, in a union hall on the outskirts of Cedar Rapids, we are like fish in the desert. Jay is not bothered, though. He is friendly. He enjoys himself. He marches cheerfully through the front door. The door is solid and secretive.

To the right, as we enter, there are three women sitting behind a glassed-in work area. To the left, on a wall, in an encasement,

Teamsters paraphernalia is displayed as trophies are often displayed in high school hallways. I focus on the paraphernalia, content to let Jay do the talking. A shiny black jacket, the sort with a striped elastic neckline and waistband, is the feature item. I would love to own it. I am too shy to ask how much it costs.

The women tell Jay that Connie has not arrived. Connie Clark is our liaison. Democratic presidential candidates court Connie. They have courted her for decades because for decades she, one of the area's foremost political activists, has been organizing. And, more often than not, she chooses winners. Connie knows how the system works. Her connections are good. People in the community trust her. She carries votes. In Iowa's caucuses, someone like Connie can make a difference. While we wait, I watch burly men with beer bellies and those same shiny Teamsters jackets pass through the hallways.

Connie is not what I expect, not hard or demanding or self-important. She is warm, happy, and casual. She takes us directly into the boardroom, where the president of the local is waiting. He wears a grimace and a cheap suit. His face is gruff like a lion's. He does not get up to greet us, but Connie is at ease, appears to know him well, proceeds as if we are all the best of friends. She smiles, jokes, and laughs. The president warms to us. He is the archetypical tough guy who says and does nice things, but on the sly. I think he and Bradley will get along fine.

On the way back to Des Moines, we stop to take pictures of Iowa's expansive and still unharvested fields. The soil is rich and wonderfully black, like fresh-ground coffee. I pick up a clump of it and let it crumble in my hands. The wind is powerful. We play in it. We run against it, arms outstretched, just to feel its force. We let it carry us like pollen into the fields.

By the time we begin Bradley's trip, which follows on the heels of our exploratory advance work, I feel connected to Iowa and the campaign. I am happy to drive Dan Lucas, the state director, to Davenport for the first day of events. Dan Lucas is a union guy. He used to be John Sweeney's political director while Sweeney was still running the Service Employees International Union, before Sweeney became president of the AFL-CIO. Dan wears a beret, swears, grits his teeth, and is a devoted Francophile. At meetings, as he warns of the difficult, lonely months that lay ahead, as he directs us to pop our heads out of the bunkers and shoot them in the ankles, he inserts the occasional *pourquoi pas* and *mais oui.*

While we drive east on Interstate 80 toward Davenport, he asks to look through my compact discs. He chooses Michael Jackson's *Thriller*, blasts it, and sings along. Then he puts in *Blue* by Joni Mitchell. He tells me that last night he played her song "River" and cried. His wife has been sick.

The town hall meeting in Davenport, one of my events, is crowded but also a bit chaotic. I stand about ten feet from Bradley, trying to keep my eye on him, which is my job, and stay out of his way, which is his preference. He is in the midst of a conversation with a stocky, slightly balding man wearing a too short tie that stops halfway down his protruding belly. Bradley calls me over.

"Joan," he says, looking me directly in the eye, "this man thinks we ought to do away with Title IX." He turns to the man: "Joan has played sports all of her life. You two should talk." He leaves us.

I am thrown by the fact that he knows me to be an athlete, but I suppose that good politicians are not in the habit of forgetting.

Title IX was part of the Education Amendment Act of 1972. It states: "No person in the United States shall, on the basis of sex, be excluded from participation in, be denied the benefit of, or be subjected to discrimination under any education program or activity receiving federal financial assistance." This statute, applied primarily to collegiate athletics, is credited with enormous increases in female participation in sports.

This man, though, is a fanatical opponent of Title IX. He has made putting an end to Title IX his personal crusade. He goes from political event to political event ranting and raving about how unfair it is to male athletes and about how it is ruining the sport of wrestling. Apparently, in an effort to comply with Title IX, many colleges and universities in Iowa and the surrounding states have cut wrestling programs, which is a problem that probably needs to be addressed, but not by repealing Title IX. I let the man fume, certain that Bradley did not really expect me to engage. It was his little prank. He wanted to escape and saw in me a comic solution to his problem.

On the way out, as Bradley gets into his vehicle, he gestures to me. "Do you know much about Title IX?"

I hesitate. I am anxious to impress him. I would like to say yes. I do not know if yes is a truthful answer. I offer a flabby, non-committal, "I guess." I immediately want to take it back.

"What can you tell me about proportionality?" He pauses. I squirm. I can't bear to admit ignorance. Fortunately, before I can answer, he says, "Write me a brief." I nod. He raises his eyebrows.

I have been given a chance to engage in substantive activity, to show him something other than how well I can hang a banner. I immediately fantasize that he is grooming me for bigger things, for being a speechwriter in the White House. Yet there is doubt. He might not have been serious. He is likely to forget. I probably should not waste my time.

The next day, Halloween, a Sunday, Bradley flies from Davenport to Ames. He flies to maximize his time and decides, at Ames's tiny airport, to take a few minutes of rest. He puts a lounge chair out on the edge of the runway and suns himself. When the press plane lands, he waves. It is an ode to whim.

Jane Greimann's door knocking has nothing to do with whim. Jane Greimann is a local politician, and Bradley is about to go door-to-door with her to talk with real voters about real issues. It is supposed to look spontaneous, but there will not be anything spontaneous about it. Jay and I planned carefully. We planned every detail.

First we chose the neighborhood, a neighborhood with registered voters, but not with any old set of registered voters. There had to be a mix of registered voters, a mix that included independents and Republicans but that erred on the side of the Democrats. Also, Bradley has only a limited amount of time to allot to each event, so efficiency is essential. We did not want him and a whole entourage of cameras wandering from unoccupied home to unoccupied home. When a candidate knocks, someone should answer. And when people answer, the candidate should not encounter too much hostility or, for that matter, too much apathy, because if the candidate does, then that will be the story.

The point is to provide the press with an opportunity to take interesting, sincere, heartwarming shots of the candidate making him- or herself available to responsive, polite, photogenic people with basketball hoops tacked onto their garages and lemonade stands in their front yards. But everything can't be too perfect. It can't turn out that everyone is home and supportive. Then the press will not think it is authentic. The houses can't be too far apart because that makes the underlying blueprint too apparent. It becomes obvious that objectionable homes are intentionally being skipped. Of course, everyone in the press corps knows that a door knocking involves planning, but there is a certain expectation of concealment. And the neighborhood can't be too rich. Rich does not send the right message, but it can't be too poor, either. Working class works best. If it rains, then it is bad news all around.

So Jay and I walked endlessly up and down the streets of Ames, looking for suitable houses. We eliminated people who came to the door naked and people who called politicians despicable and people who did not know it is an election year and people who yelled us off their porch and people who accused us of being Peeping Toms. Luckily, the word is that Bradley behaves well, is cooperative, when it comes to door knocking. And, in fact, the door knocking goes off without a hitch, as do the rest of the events in Ames.

Next, after meeting with an agriculture expert, Bradley will fly from Ames to Ft. Dodge. Bradley, a senator from an industrial northeastern state, does not have a background in agriculture and needs, therefore, to consult people as he formulates and solidifies his positions. The agriculture expert is waiting upstairs in a hotel room that we rented for this exclusive purpose while I wait downstairs for

Bradley. When Bradley arrives, I lead him to the elevator. The rest of the entourage wait in the lobby. It is the first time I have ever been alone with Bradley.

"How are your knees?" he asks. My knees? My knees? My mind is blank. I can't put together a coherent thought. I have no idea what he is talking about. I am silent. "You've had problems with your knees, haven't you?"

Oh, my knees. "Yes, thank you for asking, they have recovered well." Damn it, I forgot to press the elevator button. We go to the wrong floor. Other people get on the elevator. We have to go back down. I apologize to Bradley. Years ago, he must have heard from John McPhee or one of my sisters about my knees. Again, I marvel at his memory.

Jay needs my help in Ft. Dodge, which is where Bradley is headed, and the only way that I can get up there in time is to fly on Bradley's plane. It is a small plane. There will only be six of us. I am foolishly elated by the prospect of seeing Iowa from above and of seeing, if only for a short time, life within the inner sanctum.

As I get into the plane, Matt Henshon, Bradley's body man, says, "Bradley was serious about that Title IX thing. Put that together for him, will you?"

"Of course," I say.

On the plane, Bradley asks a few questions of Eric Hauser, the press secretary. Then, he asks me to run through the names of key people at this upcoming event, to run through the names he should know, the names he needs to remember. Soon thereafter, he goes to sleep.

When the plane lands, Bradley is jerked awake, and as he is

jerked awake, I hear him muttering those same names. It seems that he has been trying to memorize them in his sleep. It strikes me as an extraordinary insight into the mind of the politician, a mind that is never at rest.

Two days later I am back in New York, as directed by Andrew, preparing for a Madison Square Garden fund-raiser that promises to be huge, slick, and politically innovative. The idea is to have Bill Bradley return to the Garden twenty-six years after helping the New York Knicks win their last National Basketball Association title. The event is replete with stars. There are movie stars, musicians, and basketball legends. Andrew puts Megan Hall, who currently does most of her advance work in New Hampshire, and me in charge of the stars. We are responsible for, to name just a few, Julius Erving, Kareem Abdul-Jabbar, Bob Cousy, Oscar Robertson, Walt Frazier, Earl Monroe, Jerry Lucas, and Willis Reed. We are responsible for Harvey Keitel and Ethan Hawke, the actors; Spike Lee, the director; John McEnroe, the tennis player; and Bruce Hornsby, the rock musician. Megan and I spend days trying to figure out how to coordinate their movements; assigning people to escort them and briefing these people, members of our staff, on their responsibilities; oiling the gears of our advance machinery so that it all goes smoothly.

It goes smoothly. On November 14, on the morning before the event, basketball legends fan across the network talk shows to praise Bradley. And the event itself is produced, with our campaign's supervision, by NBA Entertainment and is replete with lights, music, and cheerleaders. There is an emcee, Robin Roberts, the sportscaster from ESPN. There are panels, roundtables, speeches, layup contests, and contestant prizes. There is the Brooklyn Youth Chorus. The culminating moment comes, though, when Bradley and his former teammates take the floor to reenact the play leading up to Willis Reed's famous basket in the seventh and deciding game of the 1970 league finals.

The event draws approximately 7,500 people, raises $1.5 million, and provides the equivalent of several hundred thousands dollars in free advertising. Our campaign is on fire. We are gaining ground in the national polls. In New Hampshire, we hold a lead. And while we dance in the limelight, the media mock Gore for some comment he made about how he too plays basketball and for hiring Naomi Wolf, a woman, to turn him into more of a man.

It is the ultimate in celebrity politics, but I am not bothered. Maybe I have become more of a political realist, or maybe I am too in love to see straight, but I do not perceive a substantial ideological conflict. Accepting help and endorsements from famous and adoring friends hardly seems like a threat to principle.

What does bother me is being in New York. Oddly, I find myself missing Iowa, aching to go back. I hate working out of national headquarters in New Jersey. I hate tromping around Madison Square Garden, an area that is already familiar to me. The work has all the tedious elements of advance work in Iowa without the redeeming sense of discovery and adventure. It is also hard to be on the job for twelve and sixteen hours each day in New York, where I have a girlfriend and where there are so many things I would rather do.

I realize, too, upon returning, why I left. I went to Iowa to escape. I wanted to escape a number of things, among them my family and the sense of disconnect, the feeling of suddenly not belonging that surfaced after my father's death. I wanted to escape my sadness and my uncertain place in the world. I wanted to be where I had no confusing relationships to contend with, where my fears about the future, about careers and lifestyle, were subsumed by other things. Flo is hurt by my desire to leave, but the desire remains. In fact, I do not even mind the prospect of spending Thanksgiving in Iowa.

This good cheer about escaping to a life in America's heartland, however, is short-lived. After five restless and thankless days pursuing someone else's dreams, after driving thousands of miles alone along straight, flat, desolate roads, I am exhausted and on the verge of tears. It is ten o'clock at night. I have been up since dawn. I am by myself at an empty Chinese restaurant in Waterloo, waiting for what will be my first food of the day, and the day is by no means over.

I drive to the airport in Cedar Falls, where I wait for Bradley so that I can send him off to another state. I accidentally give Bradley already signed books to sign again, as gifts for supporters. I discover that his food is not on the plane. Earlier, someone forgot to give him these books to sign and asked me, at the last minute, to get it done. The man preparing the plane told me, when I inquired, that Bradley's food was ready. I apologize to Bradley without explaining. He looks tired. He asks scolding questions. As Thomas Jefferson once noted, "The pain of a little censure, even when it is unfounded, is more acute than the pleasure of much praise."

When Bradley's plane finally takes off, it is midnight and I am alone in Cedar Falls, over a hundred miles from Des Moines, hours from a bed. A few minutes later, impatient and driving a steady 105 mph, I bend to pick up my cell phone, which has fallen onto the floor ringing, and look up, after retrieving it, to find I am driving through an intersection and am no more than fifteen feet from the side of a shiny red truck. I swerve off the road and swerve back on. My car threatens to roll over and over. Someone is calling to ask if Bradley's plane got off the ground safely. I tell them yes and hang up. My hands are shaking. I get out of the car. My whole body begins shaking. The night is dark. I can see only fields, 360 degrees of fields.

It has been a mad-dash existence of extraordinary highs and lows. This is a low. I have been traveling alone for days under intense pressure from a handful of different people issuing different directives to find a single space that suits all of their conflicting needs for a commercial, for a town hall meeting, for paying homage to so-and-so, for organizational field efforts. I have spent night after night on the floors of supporters' homes in tiny, remote towns where the stench from the giant hog lots is overwhelming. I have visited bakeries, factories, nursing homes, and schools all in a day. I have eaten poorly, usually in the car off my lap.

Then there are the highs. These tend to be of a playful, adventuresome, social ilk. Within a week of my exhausted, late night low, I am on a high. Jay and I are traveling together through northwest Iowa. It is snowing. It is too late to get anything else done. We cross the Missouri River into Nebraska and South Dakota. We have Blizzards, a special blend of ice cream and candy, at a Dairy Queen and drive down the darkest, most deserted roads that we can find. Occasionally we see developments, isolated ones with big imposing gates at the entrances placed randomly in the middle of fields, the sort where cooperating witnesses are relocated. We lightheartedly pretend that these developments are inhabited by Martians and drive through them searching for UFOs. South Dakota, land of Mount Rushmore, the Sioux, and the Black Hills, has something extraterrestrial about it. We take a dirt road deep into a cornfield and stand under the cloudy sky, feeling fully aware and fully delighted to be in South Dakota.

Jenny, her husband, Luca, and my nephew Tommaso come for Thanksgiving. My brother Tony comes, too, as does Flo. It is nice. It is novel. We have Thanksgiving dinner at one o'clock in the afternoon at a hotel in Perry, Iowa. Then we go bowling. I spend most of my time on a cell phone in conference calls.

The next day, November 26, Flo and my family are gone and Bradley is back. Two days after that, Bradley is gone and Jay, Connie Clark, and I are at a diner in a strip mall on the edge of Cedar Rapids. Pork is on the plate in front of me. Pork is on the plates in front of Connie and Jay, too. Connie is warmer and more cheerful than ever. She has been working with a field organizer for weeks to prepare for a big union event. It was set up at that Teamsters meeting back in October and will be held in the Teamsters union hall. We are expecting as many as a thousand union members, from an assortment of unions, to attend. It is another chili supper, and this time we are providing the chili.

Dan Lucas, the state director, is making a very big deal of the event. He says it could turn the tides in Iowa. He imagines the media doing something very big with it. He imagines news reports of strong union support for Bradley. He thinks that there are quite a few union members in Iowa who like Bradley but are afraid to go against the grain and back him and who will be given courage by this event. He pictures headlines about Iowa labor breaking ranks to support Bradley, about unions cheering for us despite the AFL-CIO's endorsement of Gore. I want him to be right, but he strikes me as a man inclined to frame things as he would like them to be rather than as they are.

While we eat, I ask Connie why she chose to support Bradley. She takes a bite of pork and tells me that in the beginning she expected to support Gore. Then Gore made a soliciting phone call that she did not like. Right off the bat, he started talking basketball. Obviously, someone had told him that she is a big basketball fan. Not only that, but he also knew that she loves the Chicago Bulls, Michael Jordan, and Phil Jackson. Gore told Connie about how he knows Jordan's mother and about how he and Jordan's mother once dined together. When the conversation ended, she felt insulted and turned off.

Still, she was undecided. Gore called again. "How's Smokey?" he said. She calls her husband Smokey, but she is about the only one who does. She was dumbfounded. Helping Gore was no longer a possibility. From then on, it was all Bradley for her. She has come to adore Bradley. She is devoted to him now.

I listen to this story feeling, more than anything, a sense of embarrassment and fear. It is embarrassing to listen to politicians make their threadbare entreaties and slippery maneuvers. But I suppose they would not do it, would not whore themselves in this way, unless doing it proved, more often than not, to be effective.

This is what scares me, the idea that maybe politicians do precisely what we ask of them. Jay Leno says that Washington, D.C., is Hollywood for ugly people. I think he is right. I think a film-saturated America is addicted to fantasy and wants its politicians to act, to extend the unreality of the movie screen to the nation's capital.

By the time the chili supper rolls around, Jay is gone. He has been sent back to California. It is the first large event for which I have been given sole responsibility. At dawn, in the morning's wee hours, I will begin event-day preparations. Now, at eleven P.M. on December 6, I am waiting for Bradley outside his hotel in Cedar Rapids. When Bradley arrives, I lead him upstairs to his room. He tells me that he is hungry. It is hard for me to imagine feeling it an indignity to serve him, but I know that I once did. He wants Raisin Bran and chili. I wonder, to myself, if he will eat both at once.

When I return with the requested items, he is sitting at a desk wearing precisely the same clothes that he wore when he arrived. He has not removed a single thing, not even his shoes. He is reading through a stack of materials. It is late. I feel suddenly very sorry for him, for how worried and tired he must be. He asks me how I like the job so far. I tell him that my feelings are mixed, but that it has been educational. He looks as if he is going to ask another question. Then his expression changes, and he says that much responsibility is in the hands of very young people like me. I can't tell if he is warning me to work hard or if he is confessing anxiety of a more general character.

I have often wondered how much of what I see is nature and how much is mask. I have felt that any informed and discerning person would ask this sort of question of a politician. I no longer bother to ask. I am convinced that with him it is nature; that there is very little of the pretense you find in most politicians. I am also convinced that Bradley is, in the words of Richard Hofstadter, "chastened . . . not intoxicated by power." For him, this is not an invigorating game. Obviously anyone who runs for president must feel the fire of ambition, but I think Bradley is quieted by the dimensions of the job he seeks.

The next morning I arrive early, as planned, at the Teamsters hall. I have arranged for someone to let me in. The event space is cavernous like a gym, but plainer. The walls are unadorned. The floor is hard concrete. The ceiling is functional, nothing more. I sit in it alone for a few minutes before carrying in equipment, bags and bags, boxes and boxes, from my car. I set up the chairs, tables, and sound system. I put the frozen chili in roasters to thaw. The roasters cause the circuits to short upward of ten times. I have to get the lighting technician to bring in an additional generator. I set up kegs, soda fountains, information tables, and press feeds. I tape hundreds of feet of cords to the floor and hang enormous banners, loaned to us by the various unions who will be in attendance, on the curtain behind the stage and high up on the walls so the press can get good shots from several angles. The Teamsters with whom I am now friends can't get over finding me twenty feet up on a ladder in clothing stained by chili with tape in my mouth and string around my knee, trying to get a twenty-foot banner to stick to a concrete wall that I am not allowed to hammer into. In fact, they keep calling each other in to look.

In the end, the room looks fabulous. Still, I am anxious. I am anxious until the people start arriving. We get far more than expected. The chili is a hit. The beer, Miller Lite, fills hundreds of appreciative cups. Bradley enters to the *Rocky* theme song, "Eye of a Tiger." The noise of the crowd rises and everyone begins chanting his name. The lights are careening. He pushes past a web of faces, grabbing hands as he goes, accepting kisses, offering hugs. Then, suddenly, he is standing on the stage next to Connie Clark, the president of the Teamsters local, and a long line of union officials.

During the speech, Andrew calls to tell me that he is sending me to Seattle to put together a rally. It is a reward, he says, for my hard work. Bradley's speech meets with great applause. Bradley eats chili. I walk him out to the car. He tells me that he can see I am getting good at my job. He tells me to put on a jacket and stop going out into the cold without one. He thanks me for the piece on Title IX. He closes the door of the van. The van does a U-turn and pulls away. I watch as his taillights dim. I watch in part because I want to relish the satisfaction I feel and in part because I am so intensely tired.

Early the following morning, I am on a plane to Seattle, reading *The New York Times*. There is an article about Bradley, but it has nothing to do with the Teamsters or Iowa labor. It has to do with a speech he gave earlier in the day about health care, and the headline is Bradley Says Ruling Out a Tax Hike Is Dishonest.

4

The Heart's Demise

He felt like a man who, chasing rainbows, has had one of
them suddenly turn and bite him in the leg.

—P. G. Wodehouse

T HE WEATHER IN Seattle is predictably foul. I stay with
Mary Tess, my closest friend from college. She teaches me
yoga one morning on her living room floor, but there is tension
between us. We find it in a space once occupied by intimacy. This
adds to the loneliness, which moves in like Seattle's rain, and to the
sense of dread that appears out of nowhere, like a deer or a state
trooper.

I expected to enjoy Seattle, but I feel cut off. I am used to the
beat of political activity in Iowa, to the singular focus of life at the
heart of a campaign. Here, where the primary is still months away, I
am a lone disciple sitting in a parked car next to a rally site, calling
vendors from a cell phone as rain beats down on my windshield.
The lighting technician is not available. The security guard gives a
too high cost estimate. On the sidewalk, which slopes steeply
downward into Puget Sound, men and women stride coldly past
toward an unrelated destination.

Andrew calls from national headquarters in New Jersey as I turn on the car for warmth. Wet air has burrowed under my skin. He is afraid that the rally space may be too large for the crowd. "Joan, you have to decide if you can trust the estimates you're getting." I imagine him crisp, clean shirted, and neatly barbered, suspended above his swivel chair, stuck halfway between sitting and standing. "You were hired to make sure that the candidate doesn't walk into a half-empty room." I reach for the dashboard to turn up the heat. "Remember, we don't know when or if Bradley will return to Washington. This may be it." I reassure him and, shivering slightly, hang up.

Then, without warning, with an acute sense of homesickness, I see myself as a nine-year-old standing in the woods next to a lean-to that my father and I built. My father should be nearby, but he is not visible. There is a stick in my hand. I hold it as Garibaldi or Napoleon might hold a flag he is planting on a conquered hilltop. Compromise and the future lay outside of me, beyond my young body and head of knotty light brown hair. Politics and political principles are a world away.

The local organizers, all volunteers, lobbied hard for this event and say that a thousand people is a conservative estimate. It is easy, though, to miscalculate the difficulty of building a crowd. The space they have chosen would need at least a thousand people to look full. Eight hundred would not be enough. Five hundred would be like shrimp in a whale's stomach. A campaign can build the biggest, most enthusiastic crowd of supporters a city has ever seen, but if the space is too large, then all is lost. Advance people exist to make sure this does not happen, to make sure the media get shots of colorful, energized rooms that overflow like ample breasts from the tops of low-cut dresses.

The alternative is a smaller space on the first floor of the same building, but it can safely hold no more than four hundred people. If the local organizers have estimated correctly, then this leaves a thousand potential voters stuck outside in the rain. It is better, though, to have a thousand voters stuck in the rain than to have a single shot on the news of a poorly attended rally. This is the unsatisfactory reality of politics. The smaller room, in spite of its drop ceilings, harsh light, and limited occupancy, will have to do.

The local organizers resent the decision, the implied mistrust, the stolen opportunity. They imagined the larger space filled from its balconies to its pews with chanting Bradley supporters. They imagined presenting Bradley with the gift of an adoring city. I try to explain. I know that I will agonize.

On December 10, the day before the rally, I eat lunch sitting down. I rarely did this in Iowa. At four o'clock, I drive toward the site of a fund-raiser Bradley will visit after the rally, before he dashes back to the airport. In the trunk of my car lie hundreds of hand-painted signs, political props ready for distribution.

Roger Ailes, media adviser to a long line of conservative presidents starting with Richard Nixon, once said that there are three ways to get coverage: gaffes, attacks, and good visuals. Of course, you try to avoid gaffes. Attacking works, but Bradley, like Bartleby the Scrivener, keeps saying that he would prefer not to. This leaves good visuals, so you give the media as many as you can. You paint red, white, and blue signs that say things like MADLY FOR BRADLEY.

You paint both sides to be sure that they are missed by neither the candidate nor the cameras. Then, on the sly, you distribute them to members of the audience who agree to lift them above the heads of an applauding crowd.

There is a steel-gray lake to my left. Its surface is perforated by rain. To my right, perched high above the road, are mansions. In one of these mansions, preparations for Bradley's fund-raiser are under way. I lean over the passenger seat, trying to look up through the rain at street numbers. I glance at a map. My phone rings. Distracted, fumbling to answer it, I swerve across lanes straight toward a beautifully broad and green tree. I swerve back and the tree disappears.

The hazardous little cell phone is still in my hand. Someone, a distant muffled voice, is calling to me. It is a local organizer. He is certain that we chose the wrong space. Far more than a thousand people will come, he says. His voice hardens in my ear like molten guilt. The air thickens with fault and responsibility. I try to remember when my world began to revolve so completely around the success of Bill Bradley, but before I can give it thought, I hear the hum of call waiting and answer it. The rally has been canceled. Bradley has had a series of heart palpitations and, after a visit to the hospital, has been told to take a day of rest. The trip to Seattle is off. It is postponed indefinitely.

The next morning, the morning of the event, I stand outside the site explaining to those who have not already heard. Most, though, have heard. When the story broke, it was plastered on television screens across the country. A day later, the media still swarm and feed. I can almost see our blood in the water as it dilutes amid circling fins.

The hand-painted signs, our proposed good visuals, lose to a gaffe. In *Presidential Campaigns*, Paul F. Boller, Jr. recalled Roger Ailes's "orchestra pit" theory of politics. "If you have two guys onstage and one guy says, 'I have a solution to the Middle East problem,' and the other guy falls in the orchestra pit, who do you think is going to be on the evening news?" Attacks and good visuals are effective, but gaffes steal the show.

And this was, or so I gather, a gaffe. The politically wise say that our campaign handled the situation badly. They say that we should have told the media about the condition long ago; that we should have issued an overall health report while things were going well, while Bradley was in a position to show his strength and vigor. Then the story would have been ours to control. We waited, though, we left things to chance, and circumstance has forced us into an untimely disclosure. Now our campaign is in a bad position. Now the front page of *The New York Times* reads BRADLEY MISSES EVENT FOR CHECK OF HEART BEAT.

This is the political reality, but I keep returning, with a sense of confidence, to the medical reality. Bradley has a condition that the doctors call a "common nuisance." There are 2.2 million Americans with this condition. George Bush, as president, had this condition. My mother, sister, and nephew have this condition. It does not even occur to me that this condition, spun by the media into something significant, will continue to spin and, like a tornado, leave in its path shattered remnants.

It occurs to others. I do not yet recognize the contours of the contemporary political mishap. Headlines, sound bites, and flashing images on the television screen shape public impression. And public impression congeals against a candidate who appears fragile the way phlegm congeals on a sidewalk.

I have a free afternoon before my flight back to Iowa. Mary Tess takes me to a park on the outskirts of the city where she has a part-time job leading nature walks. If we are lucky, we will see salmon swimming upriver to spawn. It is the right time of year. Mary Tess tells me the river is man-made, a human fabrication built to rejuvenate a vulnerable population of fish.

We do not see any salmon on their way upriver. There are no large, healthy pink fish shooting out of the depths over sparkling blue waterfalls. There are no silky forms hurling themselves through bubbling rapids. There are only the decaying carcasses of salmon that have already spawned floating in eddies at the river's edge.

I return to Iowa and a week passes. During this week, there is a fall in fortunes and a shift of gears, set off perhaps by the story of Bradley's heart palpitation, which lingers at our door. John McCain is the new darling of the media. The wave of positive coverage has ebbed. Our campaign, once lauded as unconventional, loses mystique as Bradley, reputedly above the fray, goes on the offensive and as staff are fired and shuffled.

Andrew is no longer my boss, no longer the national advance director. This I have not been told, but this I can clearly infer. It would seem that he now holds a parallel position, one of equal weight, one that he would by no means have chosen. Sean Gagen has been hired to "assist" Dan Lucas, the Iowa State director, but he makes unilateral decisions with authority granted him by people above, by people who gently and dishonestly insist that Sean Gagen will make no unilateral decisions. Lies can be kind, but a confused staff is left to choose between conflicting directives from men and women of perceived authority and men and women of title. There is no clear chain of command.

I know that it is routine, unremarkable. Campaigns are cyclical; momentum shifts. Firing, shuffling, expanding are a part of life's rhythm, the inevitable cadence of movement and progress. But I am afraid of power politics. I am afraid that it, a temptress displaying power's luscious curves, will seduce our campaign, if it weakens, into the anonymity and blandness of life, where what is right is sacrificed to what works.

Every day more people flow into our little Iowa office. Some of the arrivals are long overdue. Others are political specialists with unknown allegiances. They are not crusaders. They get paid large sums. They waited before coming on board. They have been invited because someone on top is losing confidence, is afraid. They come in droves. They come to tug on the string that binds us. I hate them and their expedient habits, their uncomplicated smiles, their poised pragmatism. I want to stop them from dampening our love for Bradley and our firm, if impossible, hope with their sobering years of experience.

Campaigns bring all sorts. They bring the warriors of high intention, the young and personally ambitious, the old and professionally resigned, the lonely and the restless, the creatures of habit, the adrenaline addicts, and the hard-nosed realists. This campaign has, more than anything, the warriors of high intention, who believe in fairy tales and the mercy of God, who are ready for battle and full of hope. But the inevitable happens as more and more people insert themselves into Bradley's circle. The messianic fervor thins, and as it thins, the power struggles, both petty and significant, thicken.

We all snatch at power. Politics just makes us snatch more ardently and habitually, because power seems so close, so attainable. I snatch without understanding what compels me, wishing I had strength to resist. George Orwell wrote, "The object of power is power." John Adams wrote, "Power naturally grows . . . because human passions are insatiable." Of our Founding Fathers, Richard Hofstadter wrote, "Since man was an unchangeable creature of self-interest, it would not do to leave anything to his capacity for restraint. It was too much to expect that vice could be checked by virtue . . ."

Through it all, someone on top pulls strings, and the strings and the strung, webbed, knotted, and intertwined, endlessly respond in contradictory ways. The Iowa campaign office becomes the sloppy, confused, and disconcerted gathering that I have been made to understand all campaign offices are. Still, I hope. I hope, believing that the kinks will work themselves out and that the heart story will fade. I hope, knowing that our campaign war chest is full; that we, once the prohibitive underdog, hold a lead in New Hampshire; and that Bill Bradley, our candidate, is unchanged in every essential. I hope because a present I ordered for Flo has just arrived in the mail and reminded me of Christmas, which is not far off. I hope, not least of all, because snow is falling.

Bradley is here for a final trip to Iowa before the holidays. In the morning, the events will begin. Now, the night before, I take my first plunge into the political staple of phone banking. This is not typically an advance activity, but Sean Gagen, hired to "assist" Dan Lucas, wisely demands that the burden be shared. He sets out, neat in every aspect and wholesome in every word, to accomplish his objectives. He is unassailably normal. He is so normal that I look at him again and again, each time expecting to discover something odd and previously unseen, but I never do. I feel compelled, against my better judgment, to ask questions of and initiate conversations with a man who is clearly busy, simply because I want to assure myself that beneath it all there is at least one idiosyncrasy.

He points to lists of registered Democrats that lie on the floor in stacks and with midwestern know-how provides instructions. Then, several of us, all phone banking novices, find desks and begin dialing. There is a script, which I follow only loosely: "Hello, my name is Joan Sullivan. I'm with the Bill Bradley campaign. Are you planning to attend caucus on January twenty-fourth?"

"No." Click.

"I'm not sure what you're running on about and don't much care." Click.

"Sorry, I'm full up with politics." Click.

"It's my wife who concerns herself with these things. Try back later." Click.

Joel sits next to me. His conversations are much longer than mine, and while they are generally no more successful, he enjoys himself fabulously. "Hello, good evening, my name is Joel Levangia and I've worked for Bill Bradley for quite some time now and would love to have a few words with you, if you could spare a moment." He leans back in his chair. His feet are on the desk. He's got a silvery grin to match his silvery pants. His conversations make us all laugh, but in the end, it feels as though nothing much has been accomplished. We've met primarily with apathy. The only reassuring fact is that our tiny sampling of voters proved Gore no great favorite.

As I am getting ready to leave the office, I ask Sean Gagen, whom I hardly know, what he plans to do tonight when he goes home. I realize that he must think me rather strange, but I can't help myself. I am still searching for that one idiosyncrasy. He looks up and pauses for a moment before answering. I expect him to tell me, in so many words, that he will do push-ups, brush his teeth, and go to bed. He says, however, that late at night he spends hours watching a television channel devoted exclusively to country music videos. I have finally asked the right question. I smile.

As I drive home to my Des Moines apartment, Megan Hall, fellow advance person, calls me from a bar in New Hampshire. It is a little before midnight. There are no other cars on the road. I look up at the sky, which is dark and low, and think of lying, head and all, under a thick blanket, as children sometimes do or as one does on cold winter nights, and I feel an extraordinary sense of warmth. Megan is with Jay Carson and a few members of the New Hampshire field staff, who can be heard in the background sending their merry hellos.

Megan has a story to tell me about Bradley and McCain's joint appearance, which recently took place in New Hampshire and which Megan advanced. I watched it on television. It drew

enormous media coverage. Two insurgent candidates from opposing parties joined hands to promote campaign finance reform. On a
bitter December day, McCain, a Republican hopeful, George W.
Bush's strongest challenger, stood on stage with Bradley, and
together they pledged to fight for a ban on soft money. The event
was received stupendously. The only problem was that Bradley did
not line up well with McCain. Bradley has an insurgent's platform
but not an insurgent's personality. McCain has an insurgent's
personality but not an insurgent's platform. Unfortunately, in
presidential politics, platforms have difficulty competing with
personalities; image often trumps substance.

According to Megan, there was a controversy surrounding the
staging at this event, and as an advance person, she was immersed
in issues of staging. The Bradley campaign thought it would be
better to have the two candidates standing at podiums. McCain's
staff wanted the candidates seated. The McCain staff was concerned about the issue of height.

It is widely accepted that on television the taller candidate,
appearing more presidential, has a distinct advantage over the shorter
candidate. McCain, being a short man, would not benefit from
standing on the same stage as Bradley, a man who is six feet five.
McCain's staff wanted the two candidates seated behind a table.
They wanted to diminish visible differences in height. They understood that in what writer David Halberstam called the era of high-
powered, big-budget oversell, the public response is to the image,
not to the individual. They understood that what is projected is
often, perhaps even usually, far more important than what is actually
there. They also understood, however, that the candidate handshake

would be the image of the day, the image in the papers and on the evening news, and they acknowledged that a handshake over a table would be awkward, that it would be best visually for the candidates to meet somewhere in between two podiums for the handshake.

The two campaigns agreed to a table-podium combination. First the candidates would stand behind podiums – Bradley on his own two feet and McCain on a footstool. Then they would approach a table to sign a pledge. Finally they would shake hands while standing in full view of the cameras.

It was supposed to be a friendly sort of affair, and for the most part, it was. The two campaigns split the costs. The Bradley staff took responsibility for the sound system. The McCain staff took responsibility for the staging. Everything appeared settled. Then, the night before the event, Megan happened to call McCain's staging vendor about adding some small item to the order, and she asked about the podiums. No podiums had been ordered. The vendors no longer had any available. Time was short. At midnight, Megan had to race around New Hampshire searching for podiums. The ones she found were not particularly nice, but she made do.

Megan told Bradley about the table-podium compromise right before Bradley walked onstage. And when the two candidates shook hands, Megan noticed, as did everyone else who was watching from the sidelines, that Bradley bent his knees a bit to make the handshake look more natural for the cameras, to diminish visible differences in height.

Megan's story leaves me smiling, but the next morning I wake early with daylight peeking into my apartment through the broken plastic slats of my window shade. At first, I can't remember why I chose to sleep on the floor. I can't imagine what compelled me to put my face so close to this dirty and overused carpet. Then I look at my mattress, trivial and too soft, with torn cellophane coating, and know. For days, the twisted muscles of my back have ached because of that mattress. Night after night, it disintegrates beneath the weight of my body and I rise contorted by pain. I thought the floor might be better. I must have forgotten about this carpet.

I dress more quickly than usual because I have begun to envision with nauseating clarity troops of germs, microbes, and other tiny infectious creatures crawling up from the carpet's knotty depths to invade my sleep. After dressing, I drive to Sioux City fast, as if my sanity depends on putting distance between that carpet and me. Sioux City is an old and pleasant market town situated about two hundred miles northwest of Des Moines along the Missouri River and within bluffs, which rise steeply and unexpectedly out of the plains.

Bradley has an event in Sioux City. He covers ordinary topics and answers ordinary questions. When the event is over, I eat dinner and head back to Des Moines. The roads are icy and get icier. Sleet and rain mix with snow on my windshield. On a single stretch of road, I count thirty-seven sidelined cars and three overturned tractor-trailers. My vehicle skates sideways toward the divider. It is dark. The aspect of adventure cheers me.

When I was a child, my parents often took me through New York's Lincoln Tunnel, which runs beneath the Hudson River, and I would dream always of water roaring in, not with fear but with longing, for I was sure that I would survive. I pictured myself rescuing my parents and swimming us all to safety as powerful torrents burst from the tunnel's seams, carrying cars and trucks like matchboxes. At thirteen, you are not afraid of very many things, and now, for some reason, like a thirteen-year-old, I am without fear. I want to swing myself like the needle of compass toward the storm and pass into a universe of snow.

I begin, though, to worry when I learn that Bradley has set out on this same treacherous route. Bradley flew from the event in Sioux City to a rally in Council Bluffs and intended to fly from Council Bluffs to Des Moines, but the weather was too severe for a flight. He had to drive. He is not more than an hour behind me. I call to warn his driver. Pete D'Allessandro answers, funny Pete, who recently told me that women should be able to abort up to three years. There is static. It is difficult to hear him. Another voice, altogether different, gets on the line.

"Joan?"

"Who is this?" I ask brusquely, feeling sudden impatience.

"Bill," the voice answers.

"Bill who?" I am irritated by the interruption, irritated to discover a strange man in my senator's van assuming such familiarity.

"Bill Bradley," says the voice with boyish amusement.

"Oh," I say, smiling and blushing both at once. "Hi," I say. "The roads are very icy, please be careful," I say. There is more static. I hear a thank-you. The rest of his words are lost.

The days and events of this final pre-Christmas trip blend, leaving behind a series of images of a man in motion. Each image is different from the other, but all are wonderfully representative of him. And in my mind a story is told, as it might be told in a flip book, under the force of a thumb, with sketches, page after page, of someone or something at various moments in time. This particular flip book comes into being over the course of three blurry days and is colored by my fear and exhaustion and by the love, now absurdly devotional, I feel for the feature character, Bill Bradley.

Bradley is scheduled to speak at Principal Group in just a few minutes. It is an insurance company and the largest employer in Des Moines. The event was put on the schedule, in part, because it promised a large built-in crowd. We knew this crowd would be composed primarily of Republicans, but Bradley holds appeal with Republicans, and in Iowa, Republicans can vote in the Democratic caucuses. This is significant because most state primaries and caucuses are closed, meaning only party members can vote to determine who the party's nominee will be for the general election. This is also significant because in Iowa, Republicans outnumber, albeit by a small margin, Democrats.

Still, important though Republicans may be, I have never had a good feeling about Principal Group. In the period leading up to the event, I went to meetings with various members of their executive staff. These meetings inevitably made me feel as though I had entered some crappy, eighties-style movie about an evil corporation with evil plots to overthrow good people. I had this awful sense that they intended to screw us. In fact, once, they offhandedly mentioned that subsequent to Bradley's appearance, while our press corps was still present, they planned to issue a press release regarding a long-term research project. It would be innocuous, a bore, nothing for us to worry about. Only after some digging was it revealed to me that this press release would be the unveiling of Principal Group research strongly promoting the privatization of Social Security. Associating ourselves with such a thing would be akin to suicide. National headquarters almost pulled the event, but Principal Group made concessions.

Principal Group's building has a Big Brother quality to it. This contributes to my discomfort. There is a black marble exterior. It is the sort of place that could be expected to have very tight security, but no surveillance cameras are visible, which leaves one with the unsettling idea that there are far more than the usual amount of cameras and that these are all concealed. The temperature inside is unvarying. The bathrooms are perfectly hygienic. Workers sit in cubicles beneath colorful geometric paintings that are conspicuously out of place, like a child at a funeral. Guests are escorted through long hallways to lifeless boardrooms, where pots of warm coffee wait. There is no way to tell who made the coffee, but the pots couldn't be one drop fuller.

Bradley enters the auditorium to uncertain applause, and I feel slightly queasy. The employees have arrived promptly and waited quietly. They are clothed in seemingly identical suits and wear almost identical expressions. Bradley's speech is brief.

During the question and answer session, a man in the front row of the audience raises his hand. Bradley hops off the stage and approaches the man. The man asks for a microphone. Ushers have provided other members of the audience, ones at the back of the room, with microphones, but it appears as if no ushers are available. Seeing this, Bradley moves a bit closer to the man and explains that he is able to hear him quite clearly, that there is no need to wait for a microphone. The man says that he would prefer to have a microphone. Bradley, assuming that the man simply wants to have his question heard by the entire audience, kindly offers to repeat the man's question, once it is asked, for everyone. The man declines Bradley's offer, again indicating that he would rather wait for a microphone.

The man's insistence seems strange to me, and recalling my distrust of Principal Group, I get nervous. But Bradley, altering his posture with a lively jutting of the hip, looks up at the audience and back down at the man. Then, raising his eyebrows playfully, he suggests that perhaps the man likes hearing his own voice or, better yet, that the man has a beautiful voice he wants to share. The man, who until now has worn a disagreeable expression, smiles shyly and shakes his head.

Bradley pauses, lifts his finger in a gesture of understanding, and, as if the proverbial lightbulb has suddenly been lit, says a loud and resounding "Ah." He immediately apologizes to the man for not realizing sooner and, with a comically sober face, tells the audience that this kind, good-spirited man wants a microphone in order to sing a Christmas carol. The man waves Bradley away with an abashed grin as a girl in her Sunday best waves away flattery. Bradley, sensing the man's pleasure, gently encourages him to stand, but when the man, who now giggles happily and audibly, remains seated, Bradley himself begins singing a Christmas carol. He sings a few lines of a carol that I do not recognize, but he sings loudly and clearly.

It occurs to me that this one spontaneous act required enormous faith. Bradley trusted that these people, seemingly cold, would take his genuine, playful gesture as just that, a genuine and playful gesture, and he trusted that they would like him the better for it. He was right; they like him the better for it. He leaves to great applause.

Image one in this particular flip book has Bradley, typically aloof, teasing me over the phone one snowy night as I drive home in the dark. Image two has Bradley singing a Christmas carol to an auditorium of drones at a black marble insurance company. Image three has Bradley on the brink of insanity at the birthplace of the world-famous McCaughey septuplets.

The birthplace of the McCaughey septuplets is Blank Children's Hospital, where the fluorescent lights of a lobby ceiling buzz above Bradley's head. Bradley thinks the buzzing is caused by feedback from our sound system and, in the middle of his speech, asks that the sound be turned down. We, the staff, haven't even noticed the buzzing. In fact, we can hardly hear it. Besides, there is nothing that can be done. The lights are permanent fixtures. Adjusting the sound won't help.

It is well known to the staff that Bradley is sensitive to his physical environment. And we suspect that, in this instance, he may be more acutely bothered because he is so tall and the ceiling so low. We want to help. I consider explaining the situation to him, but this would be awkward and require further disruption of the speech. I decide to wait, despite my fear that he will be angry with me, the advance person who stands dumbly, unresponsively, at the rear of the room.

Bradley resumes where he left off, and for a moment I am relieved to think the episode of the buzzing has ended. Not more than thirty seconds later, however, he asks again, now somewhat impatiently, that the sound be turned down. Of course, he has mistaken the source of the buzzing, but more important, he doesn't realize that the buzzing bothers only him. He thinks that the crowd is also being subjected to this irritating sound and, in frustration, threatens to use no microphone at all.

Hospital administrators, medical personnel, parents, child advocates, and children look on. They probably aren't quite sure what to think. I think the situation is extremely unfortunate. I feel as though Bradley has tripped and is on the verge of falling. It reminds me of watching an Olympic gymnast do her balance beam routine, the routine with the insufferably tiny margin of error, where her head comes torturously close, time and time again, to hitting a hard wooden shaft with a heart-wrenching thud.

Bradley catches himself, though. He sees in the making the absurd tale of a distinguished politician thrown into a frenzy by a buzzing sound that only he can hear. "Does anyone else hear the buzzing?" He places a special and comic emphasis on the word *buzzing*. When he gets no response, he grins, wags his head, and suggests, with a loopy swirl of the eyes, that after his speech is through, he should consider checking himself into the hospital for analysis. Everyone laughs. I am glad that the wall behind him is cheery, that the chalkboard has colorful carvings of animals on its wooden frame, and that there is a Christmas tree at his side.

The final event of this preholiday trip to Iowa is a carpenters meeting at a union hall. I stop by to help with the preparations because the assigned advance person is new and has been working, to some extent, under my supervision. I find her standing outside a locked building in a frozen panic. She expected it to be open. She did not make proper arrangements. We scramble to get in touch with the host, to find keys, and to put things in place before the carpenters arrive. I am furious, and my fury grows when I discover that, earlier in the day, she put out chairs, despite my warnings, for two hundred people. She listened to the estimates offered her. She was told that no fewer than 150 carpenters would come and perhaps as many as 300. She should have known. There was no hard count. Christmas is in three days. Carpenters are union men who could get blackballed for supporting Bradley. Worse yet, I have to argue with her before she agrees to help me remove the chairs. We manage to get rid of most of them, but the press begins to arrive and we stop. You can't remove chairs in front of the press. It is like revealing a bad hand in a game of poker without first taking the opportunity to bluff.

Exactly thirty-two people show up, not including the fourteen staff members who are present. Empty chairs litter the hall. A union banner hangs unevenly from the wall behind Bradley's head. I can't bear it. I hide in the back room, angry, then distraught. I am a coward. I don't want Bradley to see me. I don't want to be associated with the event. I cry with my head in the sawdust, with the sound of Bradley's voice echoing off the sharp blade of a circular saw. Pete sees me cry, and Matt Henshon sees me cry. I cry because all is not well and because I feel powerless and responsible.

As I cry, an image appears on the backdrop of my closed eyelids. It is my twenty-first birthday. I am in a hospital. Alcohol, remnants of the previous night's debauchery, coats my skin like sweat. My father, once happy and fearless, lies on his deathbed with despair and terror in his eyes. He holds in his hands a large box, clumsily wrapped. It occurs to me, as I look at him, that happiness drains from a happy man much more quickly and completely than from an unhappy man.

The days that I spend at home during the holidays feel stolen. It feels as if I have stolen them from the campaign and from Bradley's success. Flo spends them with my family. She, being Jewish, has never before celebrated Christmas, and despite the excess of presents, despite the carols, crèche, stockings, and Christmas tree, she enjoys herself. We get along well, but at night my dreams are sweaty and anxious. I dream of failing sound systems, empty rallies, lost luggage, and falling banners. I dream that there is no one to find Bradley's chosen dinner of chili and Raisin Bran, of salad and split-pea soup. At the end of a week, I look forward to returning to Iowa, the way a guilt-ridden, onetime thief looks forward to returning loot.

In my absence, a changing campaign continued to change. There were six people on the advance staff when I was hired. That numbered had doubled by December. Now, at the start of the new year, there are forty. Iowa's headquarters can no longer house the computers and consultants who arrive needing desks, phones, and bottled water. We lease two new spaces, one for the field staff in the heart of downtown Des Moines and one on the outskirts of the city at the Best Suites Hotel. I am not tasked with advancing chili suppers, but rather with advancing a nationally televised debate to be hosted by the *Des Moines Register* and produced by

Iowa Public Television. I've gotten what I have wanted. I've been given a great deal more responsibility. I'm being used substantially to do substantial work. I find, though, that there is little difference in the details, only in the stakes.

I recently read that each United States senator has an average of forty-three aides, not counting committee staff. Thomas Jefferson would have thought this number criminal. As president, he did not allow his attorney general even a single clerk. Without a doubt, the number forty-three smells of royalty, of queens and princes who, while the masses toil for their bread, have scores of servants to dress and feed them. In any case, no matter what value one places on these sorts of things, it has to be admitted that need has the extraordinary ability to beget need and need and need again.

Think of buying a bike. You may laugh, but some people, even in this day and age, go to the store assuming that they can do just that, buy a bike. Yet by the time they are through, they have bought far more than a bike. They have bought a helmet, for one needs to be safe. They have bought reflective gear, an air pump, water bottles, bike shoes, spare tires, a wider seat, a bike rack, gloves, an odometer, fenders, and a lock. And this is only if they have shown restraint.

I did not, however, truly understand the idea of need begetting need until I began advancing this debate. It starts with debate preparation, which is the time set aside for the candidate's debate rehearsal. For this, I'm required to secure a space, not any space, but one that mirrors as closely as possible the site of the actual debate. Our options in Des Moines are already limited and, as I have found, are further limited by the short notice, by the reluctance of many to associate themselves with a political candidate, and by the campaign's need for flexibility in terms of the date and time.

At debate prep – this is what it is usually called – two meals have to be served, for it can last as long as seven hours. I already ordered lunch for those who are expected to attend: for Ernestine Bradley, Senator Paul Wellstone, his wife, Sheila Wellstone, Cornel West, and numerous senior advisers. Dinner menus need to be found. I need three podiums for the same reason that I need a very specific sort of space, in order to simulate the actual debate setup. I also need a videocamera with a tripod, a TV and VCR for reviewing the video, a stopwatch, time cards, and a spotlight – Bradley will be served well if he, an environment-sensitive man, has an opportunity to accustom himself to the glaring lights. I need notepads, pens, headphones, a sound system, a guarantee of heating in the building for the duration of our stay, someone to film the debate prep, and someone to handle the stopwatch and time cards.

Then there is the actual debate, and all campaigns need a well-trained rapid response team to issue statements to the media during the debate. Our rapid response team, in order to do its duty, needs two fax machines, two computers, one laser printer, and one high-quality, high-speed photocopier. It needs chairs, desks, a cooler with food and drinks, several reams of paper, a radio, and two to four people able to run back and forth between the rapid response room and the media center. It needs five phones and seven phone lines with both analog and digital capability, and it needs two televisions: one with cable and the other with a VCR and a direct feed from the debate itself.

Secret Service – Gore has Secret Service protection – needs the name, date of birth, and Social Security number of every staff member and guest who intends to enter the building on the day of the debate, and it is not as though there is some database of Social Security numbers for me to access. I need to put together a communications directory containing the phone numbers, pager numbers, text pager numbers, and e-mail addresses of all staff members who might, under an unknown set of cir-cumstances, need to be contacted. Additionally, I need to obtain radios for immediate on-site communication; negotiate with Secret Service over available rooms; find a makeup artist; plan methods of entrance and exit for Bradley, his wife, his daughter, and all of his notable guests; arrange a rally out front to greet Bradley so that the press gets the right impression; assign escorts to important guests and get them tickets and credentials; arrange for a walk-through of the site for Bradley; coordinate a photo op for the media; solidify with press advance the details of the press filing room; try to avert the unexpected by obtaining a list of Gore's invited guests; verify the time of the Secret Service sweep; identify the Iowans who will participate in the postdebate spin; measure the stage; ensure that the podiums are neither too short nor too tall; obtain the exact debate format; and find out where the cameras in the room are going to be so we are not hit with any bad angles and so the candidate can be properly briefed.

On January 9, the day of the debate, Bradley is not feeling well. Ernestine is in a panic about Bradley not feeling well. There is a

near fight outside between Gore supporters and Bradley supporters. I do what I can for Bradley. I answer Ernestine's questions. I
send the police outside to keep the peace. I walk and talk with
mechanical slowness, self-consciously forcing an appearance of
calm. This is the inside and the underneath of campaign politics.
Minutes before airtime, Bradley and Gore stand on either side of
me, ready to step onstage, each distracted by his dislike for the
other. I am present to make sure that nobody tries to pull a fast one
on our campaign, to make sure that the two candidates enter
simultaneously as planned.

The other debates have, by and large, gone smoothly for Bradley.
I watched them on television and applauded freely, enthusiastically,
with my heart and soul. This debate does not go smoothly. Bradley
appears disengaged while answering questions focusing on agriculture, Iowa's lifeblood. Gore successfully puts Bradley on the
defensive with a barrage of attacks. Gore even has a farmer in the
audience stand up and ask Bradley why he voted against a flood aid
provision during Iowa's devastating 1993 floods. The question is
not fair. Bradley voted in favor of flood assistance, but Bradley does
not explain himself. He responds poorly. At the end of the debate, I
know that he has lost and that it is a significant loss. This is Iowa,
all-important Iowa, and Bradley, in his debut Iowa debate, flopped.

I lead Bradley to his dressing room. He wipes off his makeup. I
remove the microphone from his collar and belt. We walk outside
to his van through a gauntlet of press cameras. Twenty-five yards to
the left of his van, there is a mixed crowd of the adoring and the
angry screaming from behind barricades. I had hoped to circum-
vent them, but Bradley makes a beeline. He shakes hands, accepts

praise, and answers reproach. He returns to his van, and as I am closing the door, as people chant and cameras fire, in the midst of chaos and on the heels of failure, he leans toward me and whispers in my ear, "You did an excellent job, Joan."

The next debate, also an Iowa debate, is scheduled for January 17. The new director of advance assigns it to me. His name is Tim Connolly, but he refers to himself as Connolly. This probably wouldn't be notable if it weren't for the fact that he refers to himself often. No less than ten times an hour and sometimes as frequently as thirty, he says in crisp military fashion as he answers one of his several phones, "Connolly." He and Mullen – Mullen, the advance guru, has returned for the month of January to consult – are similar in this regard. They are men who use last names. To both of them, I am Sullivan. "Sullivan's got to relax," they say. "Sullivan, why don't you like me?" they ask. "Don't worry, Sullivan's on it," they promise. I sometimes wonder if Connolly ever finds use for first names or if, by some quirk of character, the practice carries over to his parents and lovers.

Connolly is a logistics guy. He moves people, equipment, and ideas. He descends in times of crisis to find solutions, to settle disputes. He has fine blond hair that is neither short nor long. He is a thin man in his mid- to late forties who watches his weight. He wears black high-top Chuck Taylors and an earring in his left ear. He rarely shows signs of fatigue. I do not know where he is from or how he became involved with this campaign. His answers to personal questions are always brief.

Connolly masterminded the Grenada invasion. This comes up nearly every time he is mentioned in conversation. None of us knows precisely what this means. We neither are familiar with the historical events nor understand what masterminding such an occurrence would entail. We mention it, though. Then we toss it up for the ridicule and praise that inevitably follow such a provocative tidbit. Early on, I thought the story might be a creature of someone else's making; I thought it might be something that Connolly would laugh to hear. Connolly confirms the story, though, and his routine references to war get the rumor mill spinning faster.

"You never kill the enemy," he said a moment ago, not long after sitting down next to me in Iowa headquarters. "You just wound them, because it doesn't take manpower to care for the dead. The dead are left behind, but it takes manpower to care for the wounded. The enemy must carry the wounded from the battlefield and nurse the wounded in the hospital."

Connolly has been in campaign politics for years but is proud to say that he has never voted, except once, and that was for himself. His attachment to Bradley is lukewarm. He favors him over Gore only because he favors change. In his view, nothing is better than shaking up the establishment. He hates the details that are the lifeblood of advance, the dull necessity of prompt arrivals and impeccable planning. He cares greatly for his staff, especially the unpopular, psychologically unstable, and vulnerable elements, but far more than this or anything else, he cares for technology.

Connolly jumps to his feet to repair a stalled fax machine or printer. He hangs maps on the walls at campaign headquarters and next to them puts clocks, each set in accordance with a different time zone. They are like the clocks you sometimes find on the walls of banks. He monitors with a surgeon's scrutiny the progress of Bradley's flights using an on-line tracking system. He watches the tiny computerized image of a plane cross state lines, lose altitude, and near its destination. He watches the way a baseball fan watches the World Series in the last inning of a tie game.

Our advance team is probably the most technologically well equipped in the country. Connolly buys us text pagers and cell phones and laser-activated color printers and devices to check whether or not phone lines are analog or digital. He pleads with the budget office for Palm VIIs, the newest in handheld computer technology. He wants one for each member of his staff. He rents a satellite truck so the senator can make secure long-distance calls while he is on the road, a satellite truck with direct uplink capability for the press.

Connolly cares deeply about the vehicles we rent: They must all have four-wheel drive in case a blizzard descends. He tells me to lighten up when I insist that every last cent should be saved for our final media blitzes. He commissions the design of a thirty-foot, graphically complex color sign for the side of Bradley's campaign bus, but he grimaces with irritation when pushed on the subject of staffing for tonight's event or the competence level of a certain employee or the future deployment of "troops." We, to him, are troops, and like a battalion commander, he has more loyalty to the soldiers than the cause.

The leaders of our cause, the men and women of Bradley's brain trust, descend once again on Iowa as the next debate nears. They convene for debate prep at a hotel in Waterloo, and I sit through it, not necessarily because I am most needed at debate prep, but because I feel like a high school student who has been given access to the teachers lounge. This is payoff. These are the sweetmeats of advance work. If presidents are made and sold, then this is where it happens. This is where dumb candidates are taught to look smart and false candidates are taught to look sincere. This is where mean candidates lose their temper and sleazy candidates get told to dump the blonde. This is where strategies are developed and personas are molded. This is the uncut, unedited version of what ends up in the news and on television.

I find, however, nothing shocking, no stark truths or nasty discrepancies. Bradley's public attitudes and private beliefs are very much alike. I have often heard him assert, during speeches, that too few politicians say what they believe. This is not just rhetoric. An adviser asks Bradley how he as president would handle the Elian Gonzalez situation, the situation involving the six-year-old Cuban refugee who is embroiled in an international custody battle. In the latter part of his response, he says that Elian is only one of many children in need, in trouble. He says that Elian's is a moving story, but that the more important story is the fourteen million children who live in poverty in America. He says that Americans should redirect their concern and focus toward these children. None of the advisers like the answer. They tell Bradley to revise it. Bradley agrees to revise the words, but not the message. The second time around, he says that Elian's situation is compelling, that he has great sympathy for Elian and his predicament. He says that he would like the focus and energy generated by Elian to be the beginning of a large-scale effort to address the difficulties facing children in American and across the world.

Bradley is a politician who consistently refuses to kiss the baby, to play basketball with little boys at homemade hoops for effect. He refuses to say that Elian's is the saddest and most important story to hit the airwaves when he does not believe it is true. Some say this makes him a bad candidate, that he should just kiss the baby, that politics is a con game like it or not. They say grasping at anything else is naïve and impractical. They say that politics is the business of sales, and if you have to kiss the baby to sell your product, then kiss the baby.

Bradley's responses to the Elian question are interesting but not surprising. The thing that surprises me is Bradley's sustained reserve. It is clear enough that he likes, perhaps even loves, certainly respects, many of his advisers, but there is a palpable distance, a formality. Even in this relatively private setting, he is guarded and his advisers are cautious. When Bill Russell, his friend and former NBA colleague, peeks in to say hello – Bill Russell has been campaigning nearby on Bradley's behalf – I'm struck by the contrast. With Bill Russell, Bradley seems relaxed and trusting.

At the debate itself, on the holiday celebrating Martin Luther King Jr., Bradley seizes the offensive and outmaneuvers Gore, most notably when responding to questions about racial profiling. The pundits agree and, if applause is any indication, so does the audience. After the debate, Bradley is happy. And I realize that I am happy not only because he performed well, but also because I love certain aspects of my job. I love walking Bradley down the hall in the chaos, in the excitement, to the set, and I love watching the debate with Secret Service from the set's shadowy wings. I love seeing Bradley make real in public what has been practiced in private. I love that in the middle of the debate the press corps' live televised feed goes dead, and I love racing to the producers to have the problem fixed. I even love leading Bradley, unannounced, into the bedlam of the press filing room after the debate and watching the journalists scramble. But at intervals as regular as my heartbeat, I am overwhelmed by a sense of foreboding.

5

The Silence of Good People

From politics, it was an easy step to silence.
—Jane Austen

M Y SISTER JENNY and her two friends fly in like
hundreds of other volunteers to help during the final days
before the Iowa caucuses. Jenny's face contorts when she first sees
me. I am pale green. There are dark circles beneath my bloodshot
eyes. Every night, I have dinner delivered from a fast-food restaurant across the street. The staff brings it directly into our advance
operations center at the Best Suites Hotel, which is on the outer
edge of Des Moines, right off Interstate 80. I never vary the order:
pork chops, mashed potatoes, and corn. The corn is canned in
heavy syrup. The mashed potatoes are powdered. In the morning, I
eat a Danish and home fries from the hotel's free breakfast buffet.
The home fries drip with animal fat. I can't bring myself to drink
the metallic-tasting orange juice or eat the faux eggs.

Mullen, temporary commander of day-to-day advance operations, wanted to go on the road with Bradley and asked me to stay
here in his place, to make staff assignments and field questions, to

organize, plan, and troubleshoot. So here I sit in a chair by phones in front of a computer. The chair is hard and upright. The phones are in a long, straight row. There are no windows, just message boards, strewn printouts of Bradley's schedule, beeping fax machines, tired photocopiers, and droning television sets. Volunteers peek in occasionally to see if I have moved. Some laugh to discover me in the same place hour after hour, day after day. Others find it disturbing and make awkward gestures of kindness. I look at them and smile vaguely.

The night of January 21, the night that Jenny and her two friends, Kim Witherspoon and Alice Trillin, arrive, is awful. I haven't left the hotel complex in four days. I sleep in a room just a few doors down from the operations center. Stories about Bradley's newest series of heart palpitations blanket the news. Attached to these stories is a picture, taken out of context, of Bradley lying prostrate in bed. Dan Lucas, the Iowa State director, has been quietly fired for, among a great many other things, his role in a *New York Times* article making us appear blundering and pathetic. *The Washington Post* is calling Bradley, who has begun to return Gore's fire, a hypocrite and a disappointment. The latest polls, aired at the end of each devastating news flash, indicate that we are losing ground fast.

Jenny and her two friends find me in the operations center, bouncing my knee nervously beneath a narrow plastic table. The door swings open, and as I move slowly toward recognition, my sister looks on. It has been dark for hours, far too long, it seems, for any of us to be awake, and they, consummate New Yorkers, wearing black, dressed in the highest style, appear to me almost as an apparition.

For several seconds, I am silent. My sister is also silent. There is something strange to each of us about the sight of the other. I am haggard and unkempt. She is rosy and put together. Between us, there is an unfamiliar distance. I do not realize immediately that I am responsible for this distance. Then I see it. I see in her concerned eyes, in our own contrasting images, that after months of being bound by snow and emotion in a world of Iowa politics and long, unbending Iowa highways, I have changed. When I first visited campaign headquarters in New Jersey, I marveled at the pale skin and softened bodies of the campaign workers. When I first came to Iowa, I found it astonishing and upsetting to be surrounded by people with no individual lives apart from their duties. I am now one of those people, and now it is my sister Jenny who marvels, who is astonished and upset.

Jenny, Kim, and Alice go door knocking in Iowa City on January 22. They are sent, along with several dozen other volunteers, to "get out the vote" for Bradley. They return with stories, pleasant stories, stories about their successes, about odd encounters, about Iowa, and about one another. I listen, conscious somehow that their stories – the stories of these fellow political outsiders – will become part of my story, conscious somehow that their experiences will influence and broaden my own experience.

It is Jenny's birthday. It is the end of their first full day in Iowa. They want to eat a nice meal. I take them to downtown Des Moines. We drive from fully booked restaurant to fully booked restaurant. Iowa's capital city, normally dead, is bursting with a final explosion of political heat and motion. The caucuses are two days away. The media have descended en masse. (I later hear a journalist note that if the reporters and editors covering the caucuses were voting in them, they would make up 1 percent of the electorate.) We are forced to settle for a brewpub. Jenny, Kim, and Alice do not mind. They are in high spirits. I worry.

Halfway through dinner, in the middle of a toast to Bradley, my cell phone rings. The *Des Moines Register*, Iowa's largest newspaper, has endorsed us. I stop worrying. I receive the news as I did my college acceptance letters, with a sense of validation, relief, and overwhelming joy.

> We favor Bill Bradley for the Democratic presidential nomination . . . Vice President Al Gore . . . has prepared himself exceptionally well. He is sharp on the issues and can recite the details of just about every government program . . . But choosing a new president to take office in 2001 isn't as simple as turning to the candidate with the most experience or the most intensity. The task involves looking for the leader whose ideas and approach to governing most closely match the needs of the times. That's where we give the edge to Bradley . . . this is a signal moment in history. Because we are living through it, perhaps Americans do not fully comprehend how extraordinary it is. When has there ever been one nation to which the world so singularly looked for leadership? The first decade of the new century should be a time of unparalleled opportunity, not only to extend the fruits of the new technology to more Americans but to foster conditions worldwide for a lasting peace. Bradley's vision is compelling. Moreover, there is a fundamental decency about

him that would bode well for healing the festering partisan wounds that have produced a virtual stalemate in our national government. Of the two candidates for the Democratic nomination, Bill Bradley has the better appreciation of the possibilities and the right kind of leadership to realize them.

It is everything to me. It is what I think. It is what I want the world to think. It feels as if I have swallowed the moon and the stars.

The feeling fades. The endorsement does nothing to stem the flow of bad coverage. I had hoped for one final precaucus plot turn, for good fortune to come barreling out of the bushes. The plot doesn't turn. It stays its dismal course. But on caucus night, at the very last moment, Jenny, Kim, and Alice weave in a small and comic twist.

These three women are asked by the campaign to deliver a Bradley supporter in a county just south of Des Moines to a precinct caucus. They expect a person too old to drive but find an overweight man in his late thirties, sitting in a small, rectangular house watching television with nothing other than a burning cigarette for light. They have driven forty miles over patches of black ice through gusting winds to transport this man, who is no older and no more decrepit than they are, to a caucus site that turns out to be less than two hundred yards from his front door. On the night of truth, when all may perhaps be decided, their services have been thus employed, and they are bewildered. Eventually, though, they relinquish, each in her private thoughts, to the absurdity and, once done, rather enjoy the adventure of something so far removed from New York City and Prada boots.

135

The man met Bradley a winter ago by chance at a local gathering, and Bradley shook his hand warmly. In remembrance of that, he declared himself willing, when asked by a solicitous young organizer, to attend caucus on Bradley's behalf on the condition that transportation be provided. Months later he opens his door to find three women. A slight upward curl of his lip suggests to them that he is amused, happy, or, as they are, slightly bewildered.

The caucus is in a school. The man enters first, and the women observe, as they follow, that two other caucuses are being held in the same building. Bordering precincts often pool resources and convene in a single place accessible to all. Some caucuses are held in private homes, others in libraries, community centers, church basements, or civic clubs. The women are glad to be in a school rather than a private home, but Kim and Jenny, feeling acutely their own anomalous appearance, move slowly and self-consciously down its narrow hallways. Alice marches forward freely.

The proceedings are already under way. It is past seven. About ten people are present. The man brought by Jenny, Kim, and Alice is the caucus's one and only Bradley supporter. He sits down by himself, facing the man in charge.

The man in charge has a Gore pin fastened to his shirt and an appearance that grips the attention of all three women. He is of average height and clear complexion, but his mouth is compressed irrevocably into a snarl, and, more notably, he is wearing thick black glasses with a crack down the middle of one lens. As if this were not implausible enough, he is also missing two fingers on one hand, presumably the casualties of a Maytag machine – this is

Maytag territory – and has a rather visible growth on the other hand, made somewhat more grotesque by a profound surgical scar.

Jenny remains near the door, utterly unwilling to move. Alice wanders about, looking with unveiled interest at the seated participants, at the women conducting sign-in, at the display of literature, and at the table of cupcakes. Kim begins to do as she was told and hang Bradley placards on the walls next to the multitude of Gore placards that have already been posted. The man in charge eyes Kim with a mixture of astonishment and disgust for some minutes through his cracked lens. Kim continues to hang signs but lowers her head in deference and avoids, out of fear, any sudden motions.

"What are you doing?" The man in charge finally addresses Kim.

His tone and demeanor remind Jenny, who remains tucked into a corner, of Mr. Bumble, a Dickens character whom her three-year-old son fears deeply and who yelled remorselessly at Oliver Twist, an orphan in a grim poorhouse, who had the audacity to ask for a second serving of gruel.

"I am posting a few placards." Kim speaks with a composure that Jenny finds remarkable, and again she thinks of Oliver Twist.

"Who are you? Why are you here?" He reins in his voice the way a dog owner reins in a dog that is furiously and senselessly intent on seizing a passing pedestrian.

"I am a volunteer who flew out from New York to help Bill Bradley."

The man turns pale and gazes at Kim with sustained astonishment. Finally, in the lowest of tones he says, "What?"

"I am a volunteer who flew out from New York to help Bill Bradley," Kim repeats.

"You are an interloper, that is what you are." His voice rises. "What a disgusting waste. The campaign spends money to fly you out here to hang placards?"

"Oh no, we flew ourselves out." Kim corrects his mistake.

"You what?" Anger replaces what is left of astonishment. "That's worse." He pauses and then repeats with increased venom the word *interloper.*

Kim, not normally inclined to flights of fancy, is annoyed to find herself imagining this man as a midnight incubus creeping into her dreams to oppress and burden her rest. She turns her attention back to hanging the placards. Jenny, embarrassed and ill at ease, has done all she can to remove herself from view, but one can't help noticing her fashionably long coat and fashionably high leather boots. Alice stands firmly in the center of the room, her shoulders and face betraying none of the tension so visible in her companions. Their man sits alone in the area reserved for Bradley supporters. The other caucus-goers are seated in the Gore area. The area reserved for the undecided is empty.

At length the man in charge turns his attention from Kim to the proceedings, but the strain in the air is still more than Jenny can bear, so when an opportunity to leave presents itself, she dashes out. An opportunity comes in the form of an older couple, who arrive arm in arm to support Bradley but who aren't sure where to go. They're residents of another precinct, and Jenny eagerly leads them down the hall to the appropriate caucus. Meanwhile, Kim and Alice watch and become increasingly confused by the mechanics of their own caucus, which is now well under way.

Caucuses are, almost by nature, confusing, especially those conducted by the Democratic Party of Iowa. It is not a one-person, one-vote system. It is a knotty maze of apportionment and delegate distribution that daunts all but the politicians and party loyalists. There are, however, certain things that these women understand. They understand that a caucus is different from a primary. In primaries, voters go to the polls to nominate candidates to public office. In caucuses, voters go to meetings like this one where, after engaging in debate, they declare their support for candidates and begin the long process of formally allocating convention delegates who are assigned to each state on the basis of population. These women also understand that Iowa's caucuses, the first weather vane of the political season, have an inordinate influence over who is ultimately nominated.

What they do not understand is how the votes are actually translated into candidate delegates. In other words, they do not understand how Iowa's delegates are divided among the precincts or how those same delegates are divided among the candidates. There are other things that they do not understand, but these are things of a more ideological nature. For instance, they do not understand why the voting is not anonymous. The battle for secret ballots was fought and won by Progressives at the turn of the century. They also do not understand why a two-hour process that discourages the attendance of all but party regulars is permitted in a democratic country. As David Yepson, renowned political reporter for the *Des Moines Register*, explains, only two hundred thousand

Iowans will show up for the caucuses, which means that about two million more are eligible but do not bother to attend or perhaps can't or, even worse, are too fearful. They do not understand why, despite all of this, Iowa is still in a position of such political power; why Iowa, or rather an exclusive handful of the party's most devoted, is allowed to set the parameters for the nation's presidential race as it heads into the New Hampshire primary; why Iowa, a state entirely unrepresentative of the nation's diversity, gets to choose which candidates have the staying power for the steeplechase of primaries that follow. A mere two hundred thousand people, less than 10 percent of Iowa's eligible voters, make a choice, on some occasions, for a nation of nearly three hundred million. This, they don't understand.

Alice decides to ask a question: "Excuse me, but would you mind telling me how the number of delegates for each candidate is determined once the vote is counted?" Her tone has everything of the lady about it. Still, one suspects, without quite knowing why, that there exists beneath it a veiled desire to provoke the man in charge.

The man in charge makes it extremely clear that he does not feel an ounce of obligation to explain anything to her. He does not explain that in the meetings taking place, voters break into preference groups, that the Gore supporters go to one corner, the Bradley supporters to another, and the uncommitted to a third. The two sides then have an opportunity to argue for the allegiance of the uncommitted, and the delegates to the county convention – county conventions precede Iowa's state convention – are apportioned based on the ultimate size of the preference groups. He doesn't explain that if, for example, a precinct is entitled to send ten delegates to the county convention and Gore has 60 percent of the vote and Bradley has 40 percent, then Gore gets six delegates and Bradley gets four.

Alice asks another question. The man tells her to mind her own business. He tells her that he did not come to deliver a seminar. He tells her to leave him to his work. He stops short of telling her to leave the room, the building, the state. Kim, who watches silently, is afraid that the situation might, if Alice persists, get out of hand and decides to find Jenny.

Jenny sits in another caucus, one with an entirely different energy, amid three Bradley supporters, talking intently to one man in particular, who arrived as an undecided and who was convinced by the words of Jenny and this older couple to lend his support to Bradley. This was a significant event in the context of this particular caucus because three votes won Bradley a delegate. After being introduced to all present and after listening politely to three versions of the same story, Kim impatiently pulls the reluctant Jenny away.

Kim and Jenny return to find Alice sitting at the center of a rather sizable group of Gore supporters. Their amazement cannot be contained. They stand at the door, gaping. Minds move fast in circumstances like these over the vast array of possibilities. They move like the round rollers of a slot machine until they fix on a single set of variables. Kim's and Jenny's minds both fix on the belief that somehow, by treachery, coercion, or deceit, Alice has gone to the side of Gore. Eventually, in unspoken tandem, with starbursts in their eyes, they move toward Alice and wait, still unable to find words. Alice, not entirely cognizant of their confusion, begins relaying the tale.

After Kim left, Alice continued to ask questions. The man in charge called her everything from a gate-crasher to an intruder to a fool. Alice told the man in charge that his behavior left her in very serious doubt that he would report the results correctly. Indeed, one felt, as Alice explains, that the man was, with this comment, going to combust like a car engine on a hot July day. And since her tone was so sweet, so high-pitched, and so unassuming in the face of all this abuse, and since his tone was so aggressive and hostile, a number of Gore supporters moved, out of a sense of compassion and regret, to the side of Bradley. In other words, Alice won, through the wrath of the man in charge, the sympathy and eventually the allegiance of more than half the Gore supporters. It is these supporters who surround Alice and the once solitary man when Kim and Jenny walk into the room.

The official tally, once the apportionment is complete, gives Bradley more delegates than Gore. This, as the women will later discover, is highly unusual in these heavily unionized parts of Iowa. Now delegates must be chosen from among the Bradley supporters, delegates being people willing to move ahead to the next stage of the process, to the county convention. One woman is willing until she realizes that her bowling tournament is on the same night, and the once solitary man will go only on the condition that transportation be again provided. Somehow, though, the women win tentative agreements from a tentative few to attend the county convention.

On the ride back to his house, the man explains to the three women that none of the Gore supporters were particularly attached to their candidate in the first place. They were being paid overtime by their union to toe the avowed political line. It is, according to the man, common practice in these parts of Iowa.

After the man is deposited, the women no longer have cause for containing their amazement. This process is arbitrary, disorganized, and unprofessional, they exclaim. Their exclamations are continuous and overlapping. Nods of agreement are offered all around. They are unanimously outraged. They wonder why this sort of injustice is not more widely publicized. They can't believe that the nation has so long tolerated a system that lends itself to such corruption.

As the women get closer to Des Moines, they remind themselves of the delegates they have won. They wonder if any official results have been reported. They return to a sense of hope, as if returning might improve the actual outcome. They agree to celebrate anticipated successes with a bottle of Veuve Clicquot.

We meet at the Hotel Fort Des Moines, site of the campaign's official caucus-night activities. I have been wandering around the hotel in a stupefied haze, devoid of objective ever since my own caucus – I decided to vote in the Iowa caucuses, rather than the New York primary. It is being said already that we lost. This, though, is no surprise. Bradley never hoped to win, not in Iowa, not as an insurgent. Bradley hoped only to beat the odds, to defy expectations. The media helped to determine these odds, these expectations, and now the media get to report on whether or not we met them.

While waiting for these reports, I go with my sister and her friends to the hotel's restaurant. They tell me their story. I laugh. I feel strangely reassured, as though I've been given the perfect, condensed explanation for our losses should the media deem our losses substantial. These are Iowa caucuses in a nutshell, I want to say. I want to complain about low voter turnout and about how little the decisions of those who do turn out relate to substance. Then it occurs to me, and I'm suddenly ashamed of my memory's lapses, that earlier tonight for the first time in my life I voted in something other than a general election.

My interest in politics and sense of urgency about political involvement so encompasses me that I almost forgot how recently it began. I look around the restaurant, which is now filled with campaign workers. I think of Flo, who cries when she votes. I think of my father, who wrote so often to our senators and congressman while I was growing up, who was anxious always to serve on juries. I try to remember if he and I ever had any conversations about voting. None come to mind.

All that comes to mind is a certain cold morning during my first year in college. It was early. I was headed toward the bathroom in the hall. I opened my dorm-room door. Outside on the floor at my feet was a *New York Times* with my name written across a white label at the top. My father had purchased a subscription for me. I had just turned eighteen.

I start to wonder, as I think of that morning, about the process of becoming a voter. Statistics indicate that the older we get, the more likely we are to vote. Maybe it is a gradual process. Maybe, as we mature, as the details of our own life appear to us in better perspective, we take more of an interest in politics. Or maybe we remain passive, and an awareness grows in us. Or maybe it is not a process at all. Maybe there are single moments of political awakening brought on by change, by individuals, by war, by wealth, or by need. In any case, I find myself promising, childish though it seems, to never again stay at home on Election Day.

The United States has on average the lowest voter turnout among the world's mature democracies. Less than 30 percent of those eligible voted in our last presidential primaries. Less than 50 percent voted in our last presidential election. Clinton was reelected with the support of fewer than one in four of our country's eligible voters. Turnout for off-year elections, meaning national elections with only congressional candidates, is, of course, worse. It seems that our democracy has, in many ways, ceased to be democratic insofar as we, the people of the United States, are choosing more and more frequently not to vote. The reasons for this are, I suppose, numerous. Some people do not believe in our political and social institutions. Some do not think them relevant to their lives. Some are uninformed. Some feel disempowered or indifferent or angry. Some consider our politicians untrustworthy and the process unfair. I am convinced, however, that every one of us is not only political but also, on some level, deeply political.

Bradley often recalls, in his speeches, a statement made by Martin Luther King, Jr. King said that the civil rights movement did not happen sooner because of the silence of good people. I have long felt that if we lose, it will be because good people have been silent; that if people would only pay attention, they would love Bradley as I do. Of course, there are plenty who do pay attention and who do not like Bradley, but still I think that we suffer from our silence, and despite myself, I feel angry. I feel angry about a silence that I do not even understand; a silence to which I have, since turning eighteen, neglectfully contributed.

My anger is heightened when it becomes clear that the media intend to destroy us in the game of expectations. They have decided our margin of loss is a setback. They can do this. It is all a question of how the results line up with their predictions. They once predicted enormous successes for Bradley. Now their failures are being turned into our candidate's failures. Nonetheless, Jenny, Kim, and Alice and the vast majority of the campaign staff are celebratory. I have difficulty understanding why. I feel uncomfortable. I feel most uncomfortable with my own impulse to share in their celebrations.

Then I realize that they are celebrating, in part, at least, because they have not been silent, because with fear and trembling, with energy and resolve, they tried to do something. They fought their own discouragement and whatever else it is that keeps so many of us from participating in the political process. They fought the apathy, the malaise, all those things that leave our democracy and its citizens undernourished. Their sounds were small, but they spoke, asserted their right to participate. People need this. They need to feel powerful, to have the sense that they can change things. And this, I conclude in my own private musings, is why they are celebrating. They no longer feel distant. They feel powerful.

I join their celebrations. I shoot pool and dance. Later I lie in bed with lines from Bradley's final precaucus speech running through my head. "I'm not willing to settle for anything less than moving our collective humanity a few feet forward. I want to use the power of that office to open a world of new possibilities guided by goodness . . . Politics to many young people has become nothing more than winning, polling, negative attacks on opponents. That's not why I got into politics. I got into politics for public service . . . I believe everything that I just told you. This campaign is based on the radical premise that you can tell people what you believe and win."

I think, for the first time in a long time, of God. I stopped believing in God when I was twenty. It had been an excruciating year for me. I trusted, though, somewhere in my mind's recesses, that my father would one day argue me back to faith. Then my father died, and I floated through my shattered world without a soul. I no longer believed in souls. Life had convinced me that saints are mythical, that forgiveness is not divine, that nothing can defy the devil. Death had convinced me, coming as it did on the heels of that excruciating year, coming as it did to gnaw at my father's flesh, that death is truly death. I have not been argued back to faith, but it is nice to hear Bradley speak of our collective humanity as though it is dangling right in front of us. It is also nice to learn from Jenny, in a whispering good-bye, that she is pregnant with her second child.

6

Building the Applause

> To have great poets, there must be good audiences too.
> —Walt Whitman

I HAVE LEFT IOWA once and for all. I am in an airport waiting out a layover, waiting for a connecting flight to New York. Across from me there is a smoking box, a casually fashioned death trap of the most sinister dimensions. It is small, rectangular, and clear like a fish tank. It is a room made of glass set aside for smokers. The air within appears hazy and thick. Faces are obscured. The ventilation is poor, if it exists. Yet people sit breathing smoke, not only their own smoke, not only the smoke of the twenty or so people who sit beside them, but also the lingering smoke of yesterday and the day before. They inhale, and I watch with a growing sense of gloom.

It is January 26. Two days ago, Bradley won 35 percent of the vote in the Iowa caucuses. This is better than an insurgent has ever done. Next best is Ted Kennedy, who in 1980 got 31 percent against Jimmy Carter, then the sitting president. Bradley got 35 percent even though the Iowa caucuses have always treated insurgents poorly, even though our campaign, still unknown to most, arrived in Iowa only last year. Gore had the endorsement of the AFL-CIO in a state where labor does much of the voting. Gore had the president and Democratic machinery standing staunchly by his side. Yet the voters of Iowa gave Bradley 35 percent of their vote.

Bradley beat the odds. Bradley proved broad appeal. Bradley sent a strong message to entrenched power. This could have been the story. We could have gone into New Hampshire with "winner" written all over us. In 1984, when Gary Hart took 16 percent of the vote against Walter Mondale, the headlines were, according to *The Almanac of American Politics 2000*, GARY HART SURGE! But the press, spinning frantically like Charlotte the spider, can spin the death of whomever it pleases, and at the moment, it is trying to spin our death. It is saying that 35 percent spells failure. We are caught like a fly in a knotty, sticky web, struggling to get free before being devoured.

This is a gross simplification, of course. Mine is the perspective of someone deeply partial, deeply disappointed. A few months down the road, I may feel more forgiving, I may find fault in other corners. Already, I can see that we raised expectations by devoting so many resources to Iowa. John McCain, who skipped the state entirely, might have had the right idea.

Still, the media have choices, and they're choosing to give us a "can't win" image. Maybe they have a hankering for a new story and see John McCain as the plumpest pick. Maybe they think that there's room for only one insurgent and want to edge Bradley out. No matter what the media's reasons, people in New Hampshire, people who favored Bradley over Gore for fourteen long and crucial weeks, are suddenly saying that Bradley is a good man, but that he probably can't win. Voters, Joe McGinnis points out in his book *The Selling of the President 1968*, act as often as not on the basis of emotion and want to feel that their candidate is a winner; they do not want to feel that their votes are being cast away. And the media are brazenly helping to pull down in the voters' minds a blind marked with the word *defeat.*

Before I left Iowa, which was only a few hours ago, I started getting frantic calls from some of our campaign's most senior people, from people who would once have passed their messages down, who are shaken by our losses. The campaign intends to have a rally in New York on Wednesday, February 2, the day after the New Hampshire primary, and they want me to organize it.

The importance of the rally grows by the minute. As confidence thins, the stakes get bigger. If the campaign wins in New Hampshire, then the higher-ups want this rally to be an articulation of our renewed momentum. They want it to be a bugle call to victory. If the campaign loses in New Hampshire, then they want the rally to answer the inevitable doubt. They want it to communicate the public's sustained enthusiasm for Bill Bradley, to communicate the undiminished promise of our campaign. No matter what happens, they want me and my advance team and the New York field organizers to build the applause. They want the applause to rise up so that nothing else can be heard; they want it to climb magnificent heights and cast away all shadow. A trumpeting explosion of sound is what they want.

It is cold in Brooklyn when we first start searching for a space. I expected it to be warmer, left my hat and gloves at home, have to buy some from a street vendor as soon as I step out of the subway just so that I can make it five blocks to the Marriott Hotel. By tradition, campaigns hold events like these in hotels, but I hate the idea. The suggested room is an enormous banquet hall with collapsible walls, drop ceilings, and wedding-cake chandeliers. It is practical in every respect, distinctive in none. The space has nothing to do with New York. Spaces virtually identical to it can be found in hotels across the country. An event here would be formulaic, a tired, half-spun political cliché. It would send the wrong message. An insurgent campaign should not follow worn-out precedents. It should take bold steps. It should make clear, with something other than rhetoric, its originality of design and purpose.

I tell headquarters that the banquet hall is on the second floor and difficult to access, which is true. I tell them that we can find a place better suited to building a crowd, which is also true. I tell them this despite the fact that these are not my primary concerns, because I know that it will dissuade them and I can't bear the idea of settling for such an undistinguished space. My heart is set on giving Bradley something much grander. It is set on wrapping him in something tall and wonderfully his own.

I suppose childhood is not truly behind a person who still has heroes, but I am not sure I want to put childhood behind me. Loving Bradley as I do is hopeful. It brings back something – a childish belief in moral imperatives, maybe – something that began in my early twenties to seem laughable. He says that it is not naïve to appeal to the better side of our nature, that it is all right to have faith in your neighbor, and that you do not have to give up your idealism to be successful. He says this with characteristic reserve, rigidly in earnest. The intent alone is enough to make me grateful. He is, as he puts it, looking for a form of connection that will make us less cynical and less fearful.

But ever since the Iowa caucuses and the negative press coverage that followed, the campaign's activity has been colored by fear, and fear breeds chaos. Instead of having one campaign manager, it seems suddenly that we have four or five. Nobody delegates properly. Nothing is definitive. Decisions are subject to scores of frightened and haphazard revisions. Grasping, distrustful hands that would once have been stuffed confidently into pockets reach toward this event from all directions. Of course, I need to consult and mollify, but I am the one who is in New York on the ground, leading the assigned advance team – the advance staff is now divided into teams – and I intend to exercise some influence.

I immediately set out with Greg to find a better space. Greg, boyish and smiling, is from Ohio. The idea of coming to New York thrilled him because it put him within reach of MTV studios. He's funny, energetic, and extremely hardworking. I aim to keep him on my team from now until the end of the campaign. He and I visit two high school auditoriums and a college gymnasium on the recommendation of higher-ups, but the spaces are either inappropriate or unavailable. Eventually we go to the Brooklyn Academy of Music, which has a room that I have fantasized about all along.

It is perfect. We overflow with enthusiasm and ideas. We know just where to put the band. We can drop balloons, hundreds of them, from the arching red beams of the ceiling. The stage will fit flawlessly in a niche at the far end. A sound system is already in place. We call headquarters with our news. They no longer want

153

the event in Brooklyn. Tomorrow we will have to start from scratch in Manhattan with only a week to go.

Finding the perfect space is difficult, even in New York. It should have capacity for a thousand or more bodies, but if only four hundred come, it has to look full. The location needs to be central so that people can access it easily, but it can't be exorbitantly expensive. Moreover, it has to be available on short notice. These are the material necessities. One must also contend with political constraints. Finally, there is my overriding fixation on finding something spectacular.

Our team of four meets in the New York field office at One Penn Plaza early on Friday morning. We do our best to put together a list of potential sites. We divvy them up, and, having found that it is very difficult to get in touch with the right people by phone, we begin making visits. We look all day and well into the night but find nothing. Most of the spaces are not suitable, many are unavailable, and a few of the bigger institutions like New York University are under political pressure from the Gore campaign to send us elsewhere.

Over the weekend, we continue to search, but offices are closed. We plod up and down the city's avenues and alleys in bitter cold winds, peeking in windows, knocking on doors, and pleading with janitors. We begin taking recommendations from anyone and everyone. We visit Webster Hall, Metropolitan Pavilion, Laura Belle, Cooper Union, Hammerstein Ballroom, the Altman Space, Town Hall, the New York Public Library, Bowery Ballroom, Paramount, Michael Jordan's restaurant, Regent Wall Street Hotel, the New School's auditorium, the Puck Building, the Oyster Bar, the Sony Atrium, Grand Central's Vanderbilt Room, Surrogate's Court, Gallagher's, the AT&T Building, Wetlands, Roseland, Life, Supper Club, Hotel Pennsylvania, Roosevelt Hotel, Chase Bank, the Toy Building, Bottom Line, Daryl Roth Theatre, and dozens of other spots along Times Square, near Madison Square Garden, in the vicinity of Wall Street.

It seems hopeless. The Vanderbilt Room at Grand Central is perfect, but it happens that Gore is using Grand Central earlier that morning, and besides, the Vanderbilt Room is unavailable. Webster Hall is just the place, and so what if, as it turns out, Clinton used it during one of his campaigns? But it too is unavailable. The Regent Wall Street Hotel has a wonderful room, but it would cost us close to $20,000 to rent it. The Bowery Ballroom has everything we need, except it is much too far from the subway.

At last, to our relief, we find Irving Plaza. It is right near Union Square, convenient to everything. The space is dynamic. The costs would be reasonable. It is a good size, and it is available. Headquarters gives us the go-ahead. Everything appears settled.

Then, in passing, without quite understanding the implications, someone mentions having once seen a strike at Irving Plaza. I want to ignore it, the idea of an obstacle, of being forced yet again to search. I do ignore it for a few hours, but I can't get rid of my concern. Finally, I ask national headquarters in New Jersey to look into it. They discover that a few years ago there were strikes when Irving Plaza would not let its workers unionize.

Now, on Sunday afternoon, we are, as they say, at square one. Flo, whom I have hardly seen, wanted me to go to a Super Bowl party with her, but the rally is on Wednesday and we still do not have a space. National headquarters is panicked. My team is exhausted and fed up. In the New York field office, which is where I sit, a fire alarm goes off above my head, just as it has been doing for days, at regular intervals of considerable duration. Building management says that they are testing the alarm system, but I can't help thinking that there is some overarching message. I can't escape the metaphor: The pulsating sound of crisis threatens to obliterate our applause.

My list of prospective locations is short, even though I added to it a few minutes ago after searching once again the Internet and phone book. The best remaining option may be Judson Memorial Church, which was suggested some days ago. We didn't visit it because headquarters expressed concern about holding the event in a church. They feared causing offense. At this point, however, we have to be flexible.

I send someone who is nearby directly there, hoping that he will catch the minister or a clerical worker. He does catch the minister. I rush over to meet them. The church, one with mixed Protestant affiliations, is on Washington Square Park in the heart of Greenwich Village, in the middle of New York University. The location couldn't be better. The main room is upstairs, but there is a great wide staircase leading to it, so access should present no problem. It's exactly the right size, with wonderful old balconies, beautiful stained-glass windows, soaring ceilings, and an enormous marble stage with wide steps on either side. The minister tells us of the church's storied past and is delighted with the prospect of a visit from Bill Bradley. The fee would be nominal. Headquarters is now far too anxious to protest.

We have three days to pull everything together, to build a tremendous event. Our first and foremost concern is the crowd. We want people lined up at the door and hanging from the rafters. With the field staff, we intend do everything within our power to accomplish this. We blast e-mails, set up phone banks, take out advertisements, and distribute thousands of flyers early each morning as people commute to work and school. We hang notices in New York University buildings, in local businesses, and on signposts. For the day of the event, we even rent a sound truck, which my sister Jenny and her friend Kim agree to drive.

The event requires massive organization on other fronts, too. We have to rent vehicles for Bradley's motorcade, fill them with gas, and find drivers. We need a police escort so Bradley arrives on time, which requires contacting three different police departments. We need to complete driving directions and put together manifests for all of the vehicles.

For the site itself, we need rope and stanchion to cordon off areas for the VIPs and the press. For the press, we also need risers, and we need an additional stage. We need hold rooms with food. We need placards, banners, and homemade signs. We need a band and confetti. We need pipe and drape as a backdrop. We need lights and sound. We need a program for the long line of public officials who will speak before Bradley's arrival. We need escorts for the VIPs, including Ed Koch, former mayor of New York, and singer Patti Smith. Patti Smith will sing "People Have the Power" and needs her own microphone. We need directional signs outside so that everyone can find their way to the proper entrance, and we need a podium. We need radios for communicating during the event itself. We need parking for the satellite truck and for Bradley's motorcade, and to do this we again need the police department's cooperation.

In addition to the regular staff, we need to find at least twenty-four volunteers. We need volunteers to carry up wheelchairs because there is no handicap access. We need greeters at the main entrance and someone in the room where Bradley is going to be interviewed. We need people to hand out flyers just before the event. We need people to stay with the eighty or so press people who are expected. We need two or three people for the sign-in tables and hold rooms. We need crowd boosters, people to walk around distributing sticks of confetti, handing out signs, generating excitement.

The day before the event, Greg and I are at Judson Memorial Church, setting up, to the extent possible, with various vendors. We are still in the church when the polls close in New Hampshire and the returns start coming in. The race is extremely close. There is a moment even when it looks as if Bradley is in the lead, but we lose.

The final results are 52 percent for Gore and 47 percent for Bradley. This is hardly a resounding defeat, but we are immediately and once again cast as hopeless losers. Bradley did better than Eugene McCarthy in 1968, and McCarthy helped to force President Lyndon B. Johnson out of the race. Bill Clinton lost New Hampshire in 1992, but it was spun as a victory and he was proclaimed "the comeback kid." Ours is a different fate. Bradley mounts an unusually potent challenge against a sitting vice president in a time of economic plenty, and the press writes him off.

John McCain's amazing nineteen-point victory against George W. Bush steals the headlines.

As I walk home through freezing rain, I feel how easy it would be to give myself over to despair. Awful passions are at work within me, but slowly a steely curtain descends. Something hardens, and my face begins to feel very much like a mask. It is as if, almost, my words and movements belong to someone else, to someone made of extremely tough material, so tough that emotions are stuck outside. By eleven, I am sleeping like a rock, as if I do not have a worry in the world.

In the morning, very early, I return to the church and move forward with preparations, barely conscious of the previous day's loss. By the time Bradley arrives, the room is overflowing. People are clamoring at the doors. The line is around the block. The great wide staircase that I admired when I first visited is full of people who are willing to listen from a distance. Bodies fill the balconies. People stand on benches and chairs. Our three-tiered stage has 100, maybe 120 people on it, including lower-level officials, basketball players, and political operatives, including my pregnant sister Martha and my brother Henry. I invited nearly everyone I know, and they have come. I find family and friends stranded among the masses outside and pull them in amid the chaos. We violate the fire code by exceeding the legal capacity with our crowd and are eventually warned even by the police not to let in another soul, but I keep sneaking them in, hoping to fill every square inch with warm, supportive bodies.

Patti Smith, seventy-five shooting sticks of confetti, and a seven-piece band with three vocalists build the applause, as does a slate of local officials and former mayor Ed Koch. Patti Smith finishes "People Have the Power," and I lead Bradley up a rear staircase. I sneak through the side stage entrance moments before Bradley. The band has picked up where Patti Smith left off. The crowd is surging. The air is hot and thick. The media stand in a great enormous group at the rear of the room, on the risers and balcony. I signal Greg as Bradley walks out the door, and up flies the confetti, filling the air. Colors fall like thousands of tiny rainbows. I can't hear anything but New York City's genuine, unrestrained applause. Bradley walks by me, through a continuing shower of confetti, shaking hands, smiling, waving his fists, and still all I can hear is the applause.

7

Devilish Paradoxes

If we see a light at the end of the tunnel,
It's the light of an oncoming train.
—Robert Lowell

AFTER THE RALLY, I got calls of thanks and congratulations. People told me that it was the best event of the campaign, and I was grateful for their praise. But already, only a day later, the whole affair seems beside the point. The next stage of the primary season has begun, and applause or no applause, the outlook is grim.

From this moment forward, it's all a buildup to March 7, "Super Tuesday," when sixteen states, including New York and California, will hold primaries and select, in one fell swoop, nearly 30 percent of the Democratic Party's presidential delegates. The intimate, door-to-door campaigning of New Hampshire and Iowa is over. In the upcoming five weeks, the candidates will be flying from coast to coast, attempting to rally support through, among other things, major media events. And if, at the end of these five weeks, Bradley doesn't emerge with significant victories, his presidential bid will be effectively at an end. In short, March 7, Super Tuesday, is, with its battery of primaries, not only the single most important day of the whole season, but also our campaign's last hope.

The thought of this puts me on edge. The prospect of collapse, of imminent failure, eats at my composure. My muscles ache. I think of slipping into a coffee shop and tucking myself away in a dusty corner. Instead I have to walk eight blocks through cold winds and wet snow.

Until February 21, which is when Bradley and Gore are scheduled to debate at the Apollo Theatre in Harlem, I will be responsible for advancing all of Bradley's trips to New York City. And this Sunday morning, after filming *Meet the Press* with Tim Russert at NBC Studios, Bradley will visit Allen African Methodist Episcopal Cathedral in Queens, commonly called Allen AME. This is my current destination.

With almost eleven thousand members, Allen AME is one of the largest African American churches in the state of New York and is part of an expansive new complex. It has, among other things, an annual operating budget of nearly $24 million and an 825-person workforce, making it one of the three largest private sector employers in Queens. Its congregation worships in a 93,000-square-foot cathedral seating 2,500, and more than 6,000 attend services each week. Ours will be the third service of the morning, and still there may be as many as 2,000 in attendance. Reverend Doctor Floyd H. Flake, former New York congressman, is the senior pastor.

Under other circumstances, I would look forward to this, to seeing the world from another angle, to seeing the internal mechanisms of a powerful community force like Allen AME, and, not least of all, to hearing a gospel choir of such size and renown. Yet the whole thing feels awkward. There is something vaguely desperate about our movements. When I listen to the event's political engineers talk with assurance, as if the event and everything surrounding it is suffused with possibility, I find myself tightening with concern. Reverend Flake has all but promised to endorse us after the service, and Reverend Al Sharpton is going to be there, but the politics of it strikes me as messy and insincere.

The people at the church aren't particularly friendly or accommodating when I arrive with snow dripping from my clothes, and Reverend Flake, with whom I speak briefly, strikes me as supremely political. This doubles my foreboding, and after one strained hour, I leave, having accomplished the bare minimum. I know what entrance Bradley will use and where he will make his phone calls, but my human interactions have been tart and discouraging. I think no longer of slipping into a coffee shop, but rather of crawling under a blanket, more so because I begin, once I am outside, to shiver uncontrollably.

Before I get on the subway, I call headquarters to update them and to be updated. I'm told that Bradley must now meet with the Gay and Lesbian Task Force while he's in Queens. Apparently there's some compelling reason why this needs to be done sooner rather than later, and apparently there's no other place in the schedule for the meeting. As things stand, this meeting is slated to occur after the service, after the subsequent radio interviews, and after Bradley's private talk with Reverend Flake and Reverend Sharpton, but before the press conference, at which Reverend Flake's endorsement is expected. This leaves only a half hour for the men and women of the Gay and Lesbian Task Force, which means that I need to find a place nearby, within a block or two of the cathedral. If it's any farther away, there will be no time for the meeting itself.

I return to the church and begin trudging up and down the surrounding streets looking for a space, but the area is largely residential. The few businesses that I find are not suitable. There is, for example, a medical complex across from the cathedral, but one could hardly ask them about renting a room for a private political event. I tell headquarters that nothing nearby will work. They tell me to secure, in lieu of anything else, a room in the cathedral. They also tell me to refrain from mentioning what use will be made of the room. They say that someone else will speak personally with Reverend Flake about our needs. The cathedral gives me a classroom in the basement. The more desirable rooms upstairs have already been set aside for the press and for our VIPs.

It isn't made clear to me until very close to the time of the event that no one ever spoke with Reverend Flake about the character of this meeting and that no one intends to speak with him. I immediately imagine how offended all parties would be if they discovered the scheme. I imagine shuffling white people, conspicuous already amid this crowd but gay to boot, into the church basement, hoping that nobody catches sight of them and hoping that they themselves don't notice my strange behavior, my efforts at concealment. I imagine being discovered by the press corps, and I imagine the headlines: BRADLEY FORCES GAYS AND LESBIANS INTO CLOSET; BRADLEY'S HOMOSEXUAL ENCOUNTERS IN CHURCH BASEMENT SHOCK NATION; BRADLEY FOUND CAVORTING WITH GAYS IN GOD'S TEMPLE.

Wanting absolutely no part of such disastrous plotting, I send another member of the advance team to look still harder for a space. He manages to secure, late on Saturday, a room in the church's former establishment, which is less than a block away and which we had previously been told was unavailable. Nevertheless, on the day of the event, we are forced to make stealthy maneuvers to get Bradley out of the building. The church has no idea what we're using this other space for; and the media, who never like to be left in the dark, mustn't learn that Bradley is leaving the building without their knowledge because inevitably they will want explanations, and our explanations would inflame their imaginations. I sneak Bradley down the back stairs and out a fire exit, to where I have a single vehicle from his motorcade waiting.

I suspect he knows little of our contrivances, and I suppose it's right that he not be bothered. A candidate must delegate and, having done this, must trust that his affairs are being handled properly; but I do wonder what he thinks, what he understands, what he has been told. I wonder if he knows of the confusion and disarray, if he knows that the campaign is at a point where, with all the pushing and pulling, it's often not clear who makes the decisions, who has final authority. He can't be held responsible for where we meet the Gay and Lesbian Task Force, but with regard to our recent and more general lack of direction, fault must lie somewhere. I don't know if Bradley has delegated poorly or if he needs to intervene more often or if this is simply the inevitable product of a campaign's decline.

He gets to the meeting and back without a hitch. But while he is in the meeting, I'm told, by a member of our political staff, that

Clinton and Gore called Reverend Flake late last night and sternly advised him not to endorse Bradley. I'm told, in short, that our press conference is going to be an enormous flop, and it is. Reverend Flake offers nothing but lukewarm praise. I stand at the back of the room vacillating between anger and tears. I want to shake Reverend Flake and tell him to not to be a coward, knowing that I can't even attest to his true feelings but resenting him all the same. I walk out before he finishes speaking, no longer able to endure the image of Bradley, which has begun to melt and blur in my tears.

Willingly and unwillingly, I collect experience. It accumulates, often undetected, forming the groundwork for my political education, the sort of education that I envisioned when I took the job. The process of becoming educated is, in other words, one that sometimes I grasp at but that more frequently seeps into me, so that I'm not quite aware of it. Yet, on occasion, I do notice changes. I notice, for example, how I've begun to look, almost as a reflex, at people as voters, as distinct political forces, who choose or not, to exercise their power, to participate in government. I wonder in each new setting, with each new person, about his or her relationship to politics, about where that relationship began and where it will end. I feel tempted time and again to ask the waitress behind the counter, the friend I've known for years, if he or she will vote, and if so, for whom – and if not, why.

Getting a political education is not, though, what I'm after, not now, anyway, not anymore. I couldn't leave the campaign with this and feel satisfied. It's not the thing that rushes through my veins, that burns hotly within me. My thoughts and hopes are tied much more closely to Bradley's success, to the success of this effort, than to any idea of education. My world is clouded and colored and lit by a belief that Bradley would do wonderful things for America, and it feels that all will be for naught if we lose, if we as a nation spurn a man, a leader of such promise, because he is dry and pensive, because his intellectual reach is too prodigious, because his suit is rumpled. There is, rather than any feeling of growth or accomplishment, anger and a sense of personal failure and perhaps, most of all, a fear of loss that reminds me all too often of my father's slow and devastating death.

On February 15, nine days after Bradley's visit to Allen AME, I'm waiting at Kennedy Airport for Bradley's plane. Next to me is a bomb squad with lurching dogs poised to sniff the vehicles of our motorcade. Secret Service has finally joined our campaign. For months we refused their help. At this point, however, we need them. They are efficient. They lend our floundering operation a presidential air. They are ever present federal agents with dark suits and unflinching gravity, who use code words and who command respect. They command it even from the police, who have begun to escort us everywhere we go.

In the early fall, our motorcade was one car deep. Now, with Secret Service and a large press corps, it's twelve and sometimes fifteen vehicles long. The vehicles are all black. They are black just the way you would imagine, with tinted windows and an air of aggressive secrecy. They are black with the exception of the police department's patrol cars, which are put at the front and in the rear to keep us together and get us through traffic. I ride in the first car, a patrol car with the lead Secret Service agent. I no longer advance individual events but rather oversee larger trips by traveling from site to site with the motorcade.

Bradley's plane is stuck in Atlantic City, where he just attended the Eastern Regional Teamsters Conference. Legally, the crew isn't allowed to fly until they've had a certain amount of rest, and we have to wait for their rest time to expire. This allows the Secret Service agents here at Kennedy Airport to sniff for bombs to their heart's content, but I feel desperately angry that we didn't anticipate this. It is infuriating to see our operation harm itself so avoidably, make mistakes when mistakes can't afford to be made. Bradley is sitting on a runway in Atlantic City while hundreds of Orthodox Jews wait for us in a school auditorium in Midwood, Brooklyn. On his way to that auditorium to introduce Bradley is Senator Daniel Patrick Moynihan, our most prominent local supporter, an old and busy man who, in the end, will also be made to wait.

This isn't the only reason that I'm angry. I'm angry because indecision has tainted the campaign's activities for weeks, so that each day the events that we began to plan only the day before change. Then they change again and again, and there is an endless line of decisions and revisions that sends us flying in a thousand futile directions. I'm at a point where I stubbornly refuse to move, to believe in the permanence of any directives, until I get verification from several sources, which puts me at odds with all sorts of people.

The bomb squad and their lurching dogs have come and gone by the time Bradley's plane lands. We are well over an hour behind schedule, and I'm seething. When everyone slowly moseys down the lowered stairs of the plane and across the tarmac, I can no longer contain myself. And since I hate the reporters anyway for trying, as they have, to bludgeon us to death, I threaten to leave without them if they don't hurry. Jon Lenzner, the press advance person, who does his best, as he should, to pamper the press, gets angry with me, and we have a nasty exchange, and I feel altogether grisly.

Later, after the pan-Orthodox meeting and after a health care event at Brooklyn Hospital, which is where my mother happens to have been born, we take Bradley to the Fulton Mall, an outdoor pedestrian thoroughfare in downtown Brooklyn. We take him to eat cheesecake at Junior's, a famous Brooklyn restaurant; to shake hands; and to walk the streets.

A day that began badly ends badly. Secret Service insists on blocking traffic to keep the motorcade in stride with Bradley, as he walks, which means that we incense rush-hour commuters who are left waiting on buses. In the meantime, Gore people ambush us with signs and chants. This is something that we prepare for when braving uncontrolled environments by carrying enormous American flags and bringing along several extra sets of hands. We hold the flags up in front of the signs and people that we want to remove from the picture, but what often ensues is a half-restrained, slyly physical shoving match. This reminds me, each time it happens, of two things: poorly behaved children at birthday parties pushing to the front of the line for cake, and basketball players vying for rebounds, cautiously throwing elbows, hoping to avoid being called for a foul by the referees.

The Gore protesters and flag holders are additions to an already chaotic scene. There is also a whole throng of tumbling reporters with cameras and notepads, and there is the noise of our megaphone. The bulk of the crowd, though, is the thick five o'clock foot traffic of downtown Brooklyn's busiest thoroughfare. Onlookers stand by and watch, while others push forward to shake hands and get a closer look at Bradley, who can be easily identified as the figure towering above all other figures.

A Gore man with a big sign shoves me repeatedly as he tries to make his way forward through this chaos. I, who am trying to keep my eye on Bradley, irritated already by this intruder's presence, grow more irritated and tell him to back off. Still, as he attempts to scurry around our flag holders, he recklessly waves his Gore sign, twice hitting me in the face. When the sign comes toward me for a third time, I snatch it, almost unconsciously, and stuff it in a garbage can. The man grabs me violently, and another man from our staff, a man with a gentleman's inclinations, begins yelling at the man who has grabbed me, and a few of the press cameras turn to take photographs of the developing brawl, and I'm mortified by how low I have stooped.

A week later, on February 21, I am standing with Bradley under dim lights behind barely parted curtains. We are on the far right side of the stage at the Apollo Theatre in Harlem, and I'm trying anxiously to see if Gore is descending the stairs behind us. Gore refused to enter with Bradley, so we decided in debate negotiations that Bradley would enter first, but I'm under strict orders from Ed Reilly, senior adviser, debate expert, to make sure that Bradley doesn't walk onto the stage until Gore is on the stairs behind us. We don't want Bradley forced to wait awkwardly while Gore makes a grand and leisurely entrance. We want a tight procession.

These details are, as I have come to accept, extremely important. They are important enough that adults with years and years of political and production experience fight over them. Adults, like children trying fair and square to decide who gets the bigger apple, use coin tosses to help bring about resolutions. For the debate at Iowa Public Television, which was my first, the tosses were no small affair, but rather overseen by the state directors of the two campaigns. The second time around, I did the honors after having lengthy discussions with Ed Reilly about our needs and objectives.

The coin toss determines a great number of things. It determines the position of the candidates onstage. If you win this toss, then you take your pick between stage right and stage left, basing your decision on where the candidate would be in relation to the moderator and/or the panelists. This can affect how often your candidate appears on camera. You also base your decision on aesthetics, such as the candidate's profile, knowing, if you are well prepared, which is your candidate's better side.

I can't count the number of times I've been asked in recent months why something isn't being done about Bradley's double chin. People ask as if it's not a bother to them personally, but rather as if they are concerned about the reaction of a more superficial public. People of all backgrounds and affiliations ask about the chin.

We, as a nation, have become accustomed with television and film to our illusions. We mistake illusion for reality and expect a certain perfection, a certain shine, that can't truly be found. We always want everything to be bigger and better, so politics answers with pandering, with packaging, and those candidates who are unwilling or unable to remold their image, who are too lumbering or too short or too brainy, fall by the wayside. We want our politicians to be celebrities, not thinkers and not statesmen. This makes the staging issue very important. This explains the advent of the coin toss.

The coin toss also determines who takes the first question. The choosing, in this case, is contingent on rebuttals and who would have the final word to that first question. The coin toss determines who takes the last question, and it determines the order in which the closing statements are made, and of course, with regard to these two things, everyone wants again to have the final word. It even determines who speaks first on the postdebate show, and inevitably there is a postdebate show. Finally, it determines the order of candidate entrance. When the candidates are not entering simultaneously, the order is a matter of concern. If you enter first, as we have chosen to do, you have the freedom to interact with the audience and to shake hands with the moderator. If you enter first, you miss nothing and are preempted by no one. If you enter second, assuming there are only two candidates, you can delay and then come in with a flourish, as if you are the grand finale of candidates.

This raises the issue of applause. You certainly don't want the other candidate to enter to more applause. In fact, to prevent this, an acknowledged problem for candidates who are entering separately, the producers usually insist, in an initial pre-airtime announcement to the audience, that all applause be withheld; but we're at the eighty-seven-year-old Apollo Theatre, home of the hooting and hollering Wednesday night amateur talent shows, where people with bad acts routinely get booed off the stage and, when necessary, get pulled off with a hook. Tonight there will be no monitoring the applause.

Tonight Bradley is entering first. I approach the producer for the fifth time to remind him that we won't budge until Gore is behind us, feeling it strange to be issuing ultimatums to graying men with decades of experience but doing it all the same. The producer wants the candidates onstage as soon as possible, and the closer it gets to airtime, the more nervous he becomes. He radios upstairs to inquire about Gore, to urge compliance. Gore doesn't come. I would run up there myself, but Gore's Secret Service agents won't let me.

Another minute passes, and the producer, obviously at somewhat of a loss, begins snapping at me about how Bradley will just have to go on, and I snap back at him about how he won't go on and about how Gore needs to get down here immediately. Meanwhile, Bradley stands compliantly by my side, which is entirely uncharacteristic and which both terrifies and exhilarates me. His mind must be elsewhere.

After yet another minute, the producer renews the pressure, urging me to have Bradley take the stage. I refuse, and the seconds grow long. Bradley remains at my side. Airtime is very close. The producer appears on the verge of tears. He is unable to conceal his agitation. He says something into his radio. Moments later I hear Bernard Shaw, the moderator, announce with that theatrical flair,

173

"Senator," followed by a pause, "Bill," followed by another pause, "Bradley."

I have been trumped. I have been outplayed. I try to remain calm, calm in all appearances, which I normally succeed in doing, being practiced in a certain stoicism that is broken only by my temperamental outbursts, but the producer and his staff descend upon me like a swarm of bees. I feel besieged and ill equipped. I don't want Bradley to be forced to wait uncomfortably onstage in front of a packed house, as if he's being stood up by Gore, but I also don't want the pause after his name to last too long. I'm afraid of what the audience will think, of how they might fill that pause. Then I again hear Bernard Shaw announce Bradley's name, and still I wait, straining to look up the stairs. Gore is nowhere to be seen. Finally I consent, and Bradley walks out.

I can't see what happens just then, but the applause is loud, and I'm reassured. Gore walks down moments later with makeup caked on his face, looking tan and plastic. He's stiff, probably with anxiety, but I'm reminded of a mannequin. I don't think that his delays do much harm, and I don't know that they were intentional, but they unsettle me all the same.

Earlier in the afternoon, I sat at debate prep in the Hotel Carlyle, praying that this debate would be some sort of turning point, feeling that if nothing short of a miracle happened, then all would be lost. Bradley seemed impatient, tired, even bored at times by the advice he was being offered. Then Cornel West arrived. I don't know where their relationship began, but Cornel West has become, or so it appears, one of Bradley's most cherished advisers. He, a prominent African American orator and commentator, is a professor of philosophy and religion in the Divinity School at Harvard. He also holds a joint appointment as professor of African American studies and is the author of numerous books, including a best-seller called *Race Matters*.

When he arrived, the air went from being fixed and purposeful to theatric and charged. Cornel West immediately began talking about the aura of the Apollo, about how character in the truest sense is revealed at the Apollo, where audiences look through the layers, beneath the masks, and give brilliantly and scandalously candid appraisals. Cornel West went on and on about how this was Bradley's chance for drawing the ultimate contrast between Gore and himself. In the Apollo, where crowds are notoriously raucous, where honesty is at a premium, there would be no doubt about who was a man of character. The credibility gap with Gore would be made apparent, and Bradley's wisdom and supreme authenticity would shine through.

Cornel West with his wild hair, wild eyes, and wild manner stood next to the always restrained Bradley, one tall, the other short. The room was full of advisers with political savvy, loyal in every way. Toward them Bradley was aloof. Then there was Cornel West, inspiring and enthusiastic, but without one smidgen of practical advice. And whom did Bradley gravitate toward? Cornel West. You could see Bradley open up with him. Bradley finds something in Cornel West freeing.

It made me think of the first in this particular series of debate preps. It was at Montclair High School in New Jersey. The whole cast of senior characters sat in the folding hardwood chairs of the audience, tossing questions at Bradley while he stood onstage with his mock opponent and mock moderator. Everything was fine. Many of the questions were oriented toward race, and since this is the issue nearest Bradley's heart, his answers were good. They began throwing mean questions at him, questions that Gore would be likely to ask if the debate got nasty. Initially Bradley fielded them well and graciously accepted the commentary offered by his staff.

Then someone asked a question – apparently there had been something in the news to suggest that it might be asked – about Bradley's father. The question implied that Bradley's father must have been a racist, because he belonged, or so it was said, to an all-white country club. Bradley called the question rotten and immaterial, and as he proceeded to answer, he cried just a little, surprising us all, I think. Nobody said a word. Activity dissipated for a minute, and people began, out of what they conceived as decorum, to have private conversations about other things. If Cornel West had been there, I suspect that he would have approached Bradley and said clever, brotherly things, about himself, about our shared humanity. And I don't think Bradley would have been offended, but I can't quite say why.

Applause disrupts my reflections. I'm still standing under dim lights on the far right side of the stage at the Apollo. I walk through a side door and downstairs into the plush red of the main theater. I look for Jenny and Flo. I gave them tickets. I see Whoopi Goldberg and Spike Lee. Part of the game involves bringing stars and sitting them conspicuously in front and on high. Part of the game is making sure these stars are seen and felt. I spot Jenny and Flo on the opposite side of the theater. They are buried in an audience that is big and full of movement.

176

During the questions, people shout their opinions with abandon. And the candidates, following suit, take jabs at each other. All
night the audience applauds and hisses and screams, forcing
Bernard Shaw to ask for calm at one point and forcing a several
minute delay at another. Bradley performs well. He does everything
that you could ask of a man, but not enough to put us back on the
map. There are no miracles.

The next day I read *The New York Times* on the way to Los
Angeles. It says that Gore "upstaged" Bradley with his entrance,
"shaking the hands of each of the three journalists on the panel and
then crossing to center stage to shake Mr. Shaw's and Mr.
Bradley's." Gore made a grand and leisurely entrance. It was, in
the end, just as we feared.

On February 27, several days after arriving in Los Angeles, I write
on a postcard to Flo, hoping to make her laugh, as if it's news, that
I'm not a serene person at all. I say to her that I'm like the tides
rushing in and out, predictably unsteady, full of life and motion,
never able to reach a level resting place. I say to her that I'm either
dreadfully low, where the kelp and driftwood, churned up and
muddy, are exposed, or else soaring as high and clear blue as a full
sea in bright sun. It's true, but it's no revelation. I also tell her that
in Los Angeles there has been more than the usual number of lows.
I write the postcard in the morning after breakfast, when I feel
clean and the world looks sunny.

By midafternoon clouds have moved in, and I feel not only low,
but also bitter. There are big reasons for this bitterness, and all of
them are tied to the fact that Bill Bradley is losing. I am bitter for

small reasons, too, reasons that have chosen today to prod and taunt me. I just learned that it's supposed to rain on our great big outdoor rally, the one Greg and I have been fighting into existence since we arrived, the one meant to occur in this very plaza at the center of the UCLA campus in two days. I just learned that the Gore campaign rumored this same rally to be canceled, undermining our long barrage of efforts to build a crowd. And I think about how badly we are already losing and, in view of this, about how harsh and gratuitous this rumor seems. And I think even harder about how the idea of such a rumor had never before occurred to me; about how I will, from this point forth, carry the values and antivalues of it with me; and about how I have been introduced to yet another dimension of the game.

I had assumed that the day's capacity for introductions of this kind, introductions to political underbellies, was all used up. Earlier, I sat through a debate formatting call. On March 1, CNN and the *Los Angeles Times* are sponsoring a debate. The call left me reeling. There was an enormous dispute, fifty layers deep, among the people from CNN, the *Los Angeles Times*, and the Gore campaign about the broadcast hour. The call ended with the Gore campaign threatening, on the basis of the disputed broadcast hour, not to participate at all and with CNN threatening to put Bradley onstage with an empty chair.

I call headquarters to let them know about the weather and the rumors. They tell me, almost as if by chance, that the UCLA rally may actually be canceled. In an ironic twist of fate, a mean-spirited rumor based on nothing comes to be supported by fact. Meanwhile, Greg and I have spent thousands of dollars and made thousands of promises and worked for five solid days. I look around before speaking. Greg stands a few feet away, talking to a vendor about press risers, lights, and staging. On a bench nearby, there is a check in a Federal Express package sent from New Jersey to pay the band. Two volunteers distribute our flyers to students walking home from class. A wind, cold for Los Angeles, blows through my sweater. I want to smash my phone into a thousand little pieces. I want to let my anger and frustration burst forth like rain from a pregnant sky. I ask sarcastically when they planned on letting me know.

On February 29, at debate prep, directly before the rally – headquarters finally makes a definitive decision to move forward with the rally – Bradley is told of a rumor, initiated, it seems, by the White House, that he is going to drop out of the race. The rumor probably started because of today's Washington State primary. We devoted a lot of resources to Washington State in a last-ditch effort to get some momentum going into Super Tuesday, but it's apparent that we're going to lose, which has set off speculation about a Bradley withdrawal. Bradley tells us that he knows about the rumor, that Senator Kerrey of Nebraska called him this morning to ask if it was true.

I am immediately grateful for the opportunity to hear his comments, but he looks down, as if he's not going to say anything at all, which I suppose is its own sort of comment. Then, as everyone resumes their activities, he mutters, "Politics should really be equated with justice more than anything else." He speaks to no one in particular. It seems more of a personal musing than anything else. In fact, I may be the only one who hears it, but still I want some hidden kernel of meaning to jump out at me. I want him, with this one statement, to give an absolute value to our losses. I find no such meaning or value.

The rally itself, though big and rain free, has no particular charm for me. I wander around, doing what needs to be done, cold with fear and concern. Toward the end, as Bradley shakes hands with the crowd, a Secret Service agent – each city has its own supply of agents – pushes me. I'm irritated, but I also assume that he didn't notice my face, didn't realize that I'm the advance person leading Bradley. Then again he pushes me out of the way, out of what he supposes to be Bradley's path. I'm in no mood to bow out. I walk back to where I need to be, near to Bradley so that I can lead him toward the people he should meet and speak to, and the Secret Service agent says something rude and pushes me for a third time. Anger, always nearby these days, comes hurtling out. I tell him to get his damn hands off me and to refrain from touching me ever again and that I don't care who the hell he is or what agency he works for.

The motorcade almost leaves without me. A different Secret Service agent, the one in charge of this particular trip whom Greg and I have disliked all along, doesn't wait for me to get in the lead vehicle. I jump into a different vehicle. Eric Hauser, the press secretary, is its only passenger. Eric is on the phone. He is almost always on the phone. He voice is even, not raised, but he is obviously angry. He tells a member of the press corps that the rumors aren't true and that there is no foundation for them. The person obviously resists, pries. Eric tells her that she should trust him by now and that it would be irresponsible to run a story about

Bradley withdrawing when it's unfounded and inaccurate. Finally, in frustration, he cuts the conversation short, telling her that the decision is hers. When he hangs up, he throws the phone against the windshield. It clatters and falls to the floor. I'm not the only one who is angry.

At the hotel, Bradley and the senior staff decide to hold another impromptu debate prep. Tomorrow is the *Los Angeles Times* debate. Bradley is irritable. He rudely asks where the food is. I do my best to answer politely. Moments later, when I return with food and some additional menus, he asks me if the podiums are the right distance apart. I say that I approximated since I had no time to prepare, and he says, in so many words, that I didn't approximate well.

I can no longer be polite. I try, though, to temper my reply with humor. I say that if I had been given warning, then I would have used a tape measure, but that as things stand, I have a keen eye and suspect – and here I smile – that I did better than he would have done. I wait in trepidation for a response, thinking of how anger and time have made me less afraid and oddly more myself. He looks up at me with a blank expression, and then he says, just as my father would have said, "Is that so?" He proceeds to measure out the distance with his feet. Once this is done, he moves the podiums a few centimeters farther apart. He smiles once and returns to his former attitude of irritation.

Anger and irritation have been as fixed a part of my time in Los Angeles as palm trees and Hollywood Boulevard. First, Greg and I got into a shouting match when we lost our way driving. I also got into a heated argument with our compliance department when they refused to put more money on our advance team's debit card, even though by their own reckoning, our team has been entirely responsible about their policy of filing receipts. I can't recall all the details, but I do recall the sense of anger and indignation. I think my anger was justified, but I suppose justified anger is the most dangerous kind. Anyway, my response was anything but professional. I started screaming into the phone about how I was out here dealing with a resistant and hostile world and about how I shouldn't have to struggle with my own campaign. I told them that if they didn't put money on the card, then I wasn't going to be able to buy gas for the motorcade and that when Bradley asked why he was stuck at the airport, I would tell Bradley to call the compliance department. The department finally put money on the card, but again it made me feel awful.

My worst encounters have been with the people at the *Los Angeles Times*, the debate's hosts, who are stubborn and spiteful. When I first visited their building, the debate location, I discovered that they had given Gore all the good rooms, which meant that the Gore campaign had nearly exclusive access to the press filing area. If I had accepted this arrangement, then the Gore campaign could have issued statements throughout the debate, spinning the debate in whatever manner they chose with virtually no response from us. If I had accepted this, then our rapid response room would, for all intents and purposes, have been defunct. I explained the problem to them. They refused to negotiate any changes. Furthermore, they would not let me walk around the building without an escort. It was as if I were some sort of thief or spy, as if the Bradley campaign and its representatives were not equal participants but rather trespassers.

It all piled up, and I started to wonder if I had gone crazy, for I was largely alone during my conversations with the compliance department, and I was alone at the *Los Angeles Times*. There was no benchmark of sanity. I began to fear, in a real sort of way, especially when I was at the *Los Angeles Times*, that something was wrong with me. Finally, I decided to have even-tempered people deal with them, people like Greg and Jon Lenzner, and these even-tempered people were equally appalled and worse. Still, I felt strange about it all until Ed Reilly, always composed, visited the building, the debate site, thinking perhaps that my complaints were exaggerated, and came back red with fury, having been ushered out, almost, by armed guards. Then I knew that it was not my bad humor that caused problems at the *Los Angeles Times*.

I did, however, manage to resolve the rapid response room difficulties. When the people at the *Los Angeles Times* refused to negotiate, even though they did not have a logical leg to stand on, I refused to leave the building and said that our campaign could not possibly participate under these circumstances; it was a threat that I in no way had the authority to make, but they were exasperating. Finally, I called Ed Reilly – this was long before he arrived and met with them – and asked him to intervene, but he was too busy with his own affairs. In frustration, I called Anita Dunn, the communications director, who I knew would be invested in the effectiveness of our rapid response room. She, always kind, was right in the middle of something but suggested that I call Doug Berman, the campaign chairman, who was likely to be available.

I did call him and felt not in the least bit intimidated, perhaps because I was so angry and fed up. He was pretty indifferent at first, so I threw my metaphorical hands into the air, but not before telling him that I would lay the responsibility on his shoulders if anyone asked why we had none of the equipment or space necessary for running an effective rapid response room. Basically I threatened him, and he was, though it may be presumptuous to say so, somewhat cowed and said that he would call. At long last, we were given a fair share of the space and access to the media. In short, my week in Los Angeles has been marked by turmoil.

Now, after sitting through debate prep with an irritable Bradley, I go downstairs to watch Eric Hauser's press conference about our humiliating loss in the Washington State primary. I have not watched many press conferences. This one seems brutal. The reporters spend a good thirty minutes trying to force Eric to admit that we are no more, that our campaign is finished.

I go upstairs to the bar. Staff members of all ranks and sizes have gathered. They are drinking, and the media come up, and no one seems as exhausted and disheartened and sad as I feel, and certainly no one's manner seems to reflect the state of the campaign. They are, I think, able to maintain a more mature distance from their emotions, or perhaps they came to terms with losing much sooner. Anyway, I can't bear it, so I go up to my hotel room; but I can't bear to sit there, either, so I walk back down and sit at the bar on a stool and feel my eyes well with tears. I try then for a second time to make conversation but am totally uninterested and quite frankly can't stand to be so near to the media, who are on what is called a deathwatch. While a candidate does well, the media watch so that they don't miss an assassination attempt, and once a candidate begins to do badly, they watch for the moment of withdrawal.

I go to bed and wake up early the next morning to an e-mail from Hugh Drummond, the scheduler, asking Gabe, Jay, Megan, Teresa, and me, the senior advance people, to call him. I wonder at first what he wants. Then, after a second, I realize that he, a kind and generous man, wants to talk with us about the future, about what we will do next. Of course, I have known for quite some time that we no longer have a chance, but this from Hugh, who has in his total devotion to Bradley maintained a very positive attitude, comes as an awful blow, as final confirmation of sorts.

When I finally make it out into the hallway, the lead Secret Service agent is there. He says, "I heard there was some problem yesterday. I heard you were politely asked to move and refused."

"Politely? Refused?" I say in anger and amazement.

The Secret Service agent begins lecturing me, and I tell him that if that agent or any other agent pushes me again, I'll push him back, gun in his belt or no gun in his belt. I'm so angry that I can hardly see, but still I can see how absurd it is for me – thin, female, and five feet nine – to be speaking like this to a strapping and armed federal agent, but I can't help myself. He ends by saying, "Fuck you," and I tell him that he gets a star for maturity, and he storms off, and I march defiantly up to Bradley's door, proceeding as planned to take him to a health care event.

Before the debate, there is a Latino health care event, and halfway through the event, the same Secret Service agent decides that the room is as full as it's legally allowed to be. It is true that there are fire codes dictating how many people are permitted in a building or room at any single time, but these fire codes, like speed limits, are meant to be followed only approximately. In New York, at Judson Memorial Church, the police department gave us a light warning, and that was after we had more than doubled the room's legal capacity. Under this guy's direction, however, a barely full room with empty chairs is left barely full while people wait outside, wishing they could hear Bradley.

At one point, an old woman with a walker comes panting up the stairs, shaking from fatigue. The agent tells her without kindness that she is going to have to leave. I turn to him and say, "No, if one person is going to make that much difference, then I'll leave." I walk her into the room, sit her down in one of the many empty chairs, and go outside to get air. I return not many minutes later and walk right past him, daring him almost to say something. Right about then, Connolly calls to inform me that, after the debate, I will be going to Missouri instead of to New York, which strikes me, in my current mood, as yet another piece of bad luck.

Bradley holds his own press conference subsequent to the health care event, and again the reporters, like hungry fish, swarm, trying to gnaw an admission of defeat out of him. He pushes aside the questions and speculation, saying, "Mark Twain put it best when he said, 'Reports of my demise are greatly exaggerated.'" I watch, shrinking to see vulnerability in his eyes. Again I am reminded of my father and his death.

The tone of the debate itself is low-key, entirely different from the tone of the debate at the Apollo. Gore, who spent five months accusing Bradley of all sorts of nasty things, who spent five months damning Bradley's every word, is conciliatory, obsequious even. He says in response to virtually every statement Bradley makes, "I agree with that." He says it over and over. It is maddening. It is transparent. He plays the nice guy. He is thinking ahead to his contest with Bush. Of course, one is left to wonder what he really believes. Bradley is also less combative, and for me it harkens back to the way he began the campaign, to the way he wanted to run the campaign, without going on the attack.

During the debate, our staff, including the entire senior staff, sits in the rapid response room watching via television. They give lighthearted commentary, mostly mocking Gore. I don't feel light-hearted, but I don't mind listening, either. Then one questioner asks the candidates from which mistakes they have learned most. Gore makes some joke that it was his much-ridiculed claim to have invented the Internet, then segues into a story about how he learned, after devoting too much of his time to public service, to balance his work with his home life. We all laugh at the thought of a candidate for the presidency having a balanced home and work life.

Bradley talks about his rookie year with the Knicks, when he was heralded as the team's savior, only to be manhandled by fans for playing poorly. The lesson learned, he says, was "coming to terms with failure." Of course this sends gasps through our room, but I think that this probably *is* the mistake from which he learned most. He thought that he couldn't fail and realized he could. "I knew I wouldn't save the Knicks," he says. "It caused me to ask myself really, Well, you have to come to terms with this. That meant I worked harder in order to achieve things. It also meant I began to see that life is not all good, not all bad, that individuals are not all good or all bad." Obviously, he tells this story understanding the implications, knowing it will echo with irony, considering the state of his campaign, but I think he says it in absolute honesty, despite its effect, rather than because of its effect.

When Bradley finishes, Gore revises his own answer, saying his biggest mistake was not being kind. With this, the sound of the debate fades, and I am in a room with my father. There is no longer much hope that he will recover, but he still wants to go to my brother Henry's wedding. Of his children, Henry will be only the second to get married. My father has cancer and not much time to live, but still he secretly concocts a plan to get me a tuxedo – something I have always wanted – for my twenty-first birthday. He has someone call the house pretending to be a cousin of my brother's fiancée. That someone pretends that he is stuck abroad and needs an available body that is approximately five feet nine and 130 pounds to go get measured for a tuxedo in his place. My father sends me.

When I come home from unknowingly completing my part in his scheme, he is in the bathroom preparing to take a coffee enema, which is what the nutritionist, the only one willing to give us a sense of hope, told him to do at regular intervals throughout the day. He is not steady. There is clearly something wrong. He can't stand properly. I tell him that we will worry about the coffee enema later, and I lead him back to bed. His right leg drags. Once, I would not have been able to support him, but he is emaciated; the cancer has eaten away at his flesh, and he feels light.

I pull up the covers. He looks at me through a half-closed eye. I haven't been able to look in his eyes for months. I suggest maybe that he has lost energy for lack of food, though I suspect something worse. I rush to make him a vegetable drink and then a milkshake, hoping one will appeal to him. He needs a straw. Otherwise, it's too difficult for him to drink. He puts the straw in his mouth and sucks. For a moment, the liquid disappears, and then it begins pouring from his mouth. I'm not sure that he's even aware of it. I throw my hand out to catch the liquid and get a towel to dry him off. I recommend that he rest, and I lie down in the bed next to him.

I can't tell if he is asleep. He sleeps often with his eyes open now, almost as if it would be too much energy to close them. He's breathing. I watch for that. I lie there for two hours watching, feeling as though I have hardly blinked, as though I am made of stone, as though I would break into a thousand pieces if I were made of anything more fragile. I later learn that he's had a stroke. He doesn't make it to my brother's wedding: He's in the hospital. Three months later, he is dead.

After the debate, which is over quite late, we go to a warehouse near the airport, where Bradley begins filming a commercial with Sydney Pollack, the well-known film director, who apparently is also a friend. It is a long commercial, nearly five minutes long, and it's simple. Bradley sits in a chair – there are no books or desks or American flags in the background – and he makes a case for his candidacy. It's just the case that I would want him to make. It's clear, honest, and without animus. This is not politics as con game. This is not about slickness or modern effect. This is about the message, and the off-screen chatter, which could just as easily be snide or cynical, which could be full of stereotypically dirty political moments, reinforces in all respects that which is being said on screen. Bradley makes his case, and it revives me. It reminds me of everything that is good about him and his campaign. He sits in a chair under lights opposite Sydney Pollack and says exactly what he believes.

During a break, Gina Glantz, the campaign manager, asks me if I am going to stick with politics. I say no chance. I say that for a while I confused politics with public service. She says that one of the campaign's legacies will be the way in which it attracted young people and excited their will to participate. She thinks that one of Bradley's objectives was to politicize our youth, to appeal to their ideals. She tells me that if I allow this to sour me, to push me toward cynicism, then part of the campaign's meaning is lost.

I fall asleep in the car on the way to the airport. When I wake up, Bradley is walking across the runway toward his plane. Matt Henshon's coat is laid over me. I lift myself out of the seat and run to return the coat to Matt. Bradley calls me over to him, gives me a kiss good-bye, and thanks me warmly. A wind with the slight scent of rain and the even slighter scent of the sea blows past. I walk to the runway's edge and wait while his plane prepares for takeoff. As I wait, I think of how our experiences always seem to be bigger than themselves and exactly themselves, always seem to be the essence of some larger truth and nothing greater than our own. And I decide that this is somehow at the heart of our desire to communicate. And I decide that when I get to the hotel, no matter how late it is, I will write one more postcard to Flo.

8

Our Better Angels

Democracy is the worst form of government except all those
other forms that have been tried from time to time.
—Winston Churchill

C AMERAS TURN TO photograph us. They have been
photographing Bradley. It is March 7, Super Tuesday,
election night. Bradley is delivering his concession speech. He is
onstage with those who needed, for political reasons, to be put
onstage. We ushered them in through a side door. We ushered in as
many people as we possibly could, people who wanted or required
special thanks, hundreds of people. An enormous American flag
hangs from the ceiling behind these people, behind the stage, and
it, like a barometer of mood and movement, swells as the room
swells, steadies as the room steadies, quivers as the room quivers.
Three other members of the advance staff and I are crouched on the
floor in front of the stage, looking directly up at Bradley and this
flag. Photographers from the press corps stand next to us and have
turned to photograph us. We are all under thirty, all new to
politics, all crying.

I know what the photographers are thinking. To them, we are
symbols not only of election night despair but also of Bradley's

message as characterized in this speech, as characterized in countless speeches over the course of the past year. They turn to us at predictable moments, when we can illustrate Bradley's meaning, give poignancy to his words.

Throughout this campaign, I've talked about the essential goodness of the American people. I see and feel it as deeply and as clearly today as I ever have. But in running for president, I've also sought to enlist something else – something I have always seen in the eyes of the American people. And that is idealism. A belief that good can triumph over bad, that principle can defeat expediency. I decided to run for president to tap into that deep and abiding strand in our national character, for only by enlisting it can we create a new politics and do the great things that still need to be done. The things we can now afford to do in these times of unprecedented prosperity. The things which if we did them would make us all stronger.

For the cameras, we are the bleary-eyed dreamers who believed that good could triumph over bad, that principle could defeat expediency. The cameras have turned to photograph those whose idealism Bradley was able to enlist.

We, the advance staff, trained to search for good visuals, have spent months pushing veterans and old people into the foreground, near to the candidate. Tonight, instead of old people, however, the cameras need crying people, and we are perfect props. We couldn't have planned it better if we had tried. The four of us are an empty hog run behind Bradley at a family farm, a bereft mother at a forum on gun control, union men singing "For He's a Jolly Good Fellow" at a chili supper. We no longer craft the story, but rather have become the story. We, crying in a packed election night ballroom at the Sheraton Hotel in midtown Manhattan, are the camera's proof that Bradley tapped into some deep and abiding strand of the national character.

Yet, as with all things, the view varies with the viewer. A raindrop can have a thousand meanings, and so can a tear. A raindrop can signal the start of spring or the ruin of a Sunday picnic or the revival of forsythia in long yellow rows or the destruction of a wedding dress or the chance to use a new umbrella. A tear, depending on the tearful, can have a thousand meanings. It can be used, depending on the journalist, to illustrate a thousand points. Tonight, the four of us could be crying out of frustration or pride or temporary sadness. We could be crying because Bradley is still willing to express precisely what we believe or because we tried and failed. We could be crying because we sense the return of our own political indifference or because we know that we have become lifelong members of the voting public. We could be crying because we are tired or because, for us, the future is now entirely uncertain.

This is not an expectant election night. We are not anxiously awaiting the outcome of the balloting. We know that we lost miserably. This is farewell.

There is no doubt in my mind that tonight we are a step closer to a politics that once again is seen as noble service, where those who practice it are trusted, and where corruption and deceit give way to truth and candor. We are closer to these things because of the efforts of the people in this room, around the country, and the millions who voted today for change. In particular, I want to thank the young people whose energy and idealism are a constant source of inspiration for me and for everybody in this campaign.

Bradley thanks the young people. We are the young people. It makes sense that the cameras turn to us, but it gives me an odd feeling. Suddenly I am species and spectator, rather than species alone. I was immersed, taking part. Now I am also looking in, as if through a camera, studying the events. I am rapt and removed both at once. The cameras remind me too of what has been impressed upon me since my very first day in Iowa: Campaigns are very often about images, about communicating messages not with reasoned analysis, but with something much closer to the surface, something more emotional and stylistic.

Bradley wants to thank those gathered, many of whom are first-time political volunteers. He also wants to give meaning to the campaign's efforts. Don't let defeat obscure our accomplishments, he says. We brought young and idealistic people back into the political fold. We forced a national debate on issues like campaign finance reform, universal health care, child poverty, and the racial divide. We contributed greatly to the tone and dialogue of this presidential race.

When the speech is over, Bradley hops off the stage and walks into the crowd. I pull my mother and my sister Sarah over to me.

They wanted to come, to see his farewell. As Bradley passes, I grab him and direct his attention toward them. He gives Sarah, married on our front lawn a decade ago, the day I first met Bradley, a kiss. It takes him a second to recognize my mother, but when he does, he embraces her warmly, smiling a surprised and grateful smile. He then continues to circulate, reaching toward people, letting himself be pulled and twisted. I stay near to him, in front of him. He no longer needs me. He no longer needs any of us, but I can't let him go.

After he has hugged and kissed hundreds of shadowy forms, I stop and watch him pass. A moment later, he pauses to hug Jay. He then turns and comes back toward me. He has an astonishing sense not only of where he is, but also of who surrounds him. He bends to put his arms around me. I rest my head on his shoulder, and I thank him. He whispers into my ear, "Joan, I've seen what a good person you are." I thank him again. It is all that I can think to do.

The rest of the night is spent at an Irish bar across the street from the hotel. Nearly everyone from the campaign is there. I ask two members of the senior staff if they think that we really contributed significantly to setting the Democratic agenda, if we really helped to shape the national debate. I get differing opinions. One says that we did beyond a doubt and points to all the journalists and pundits who are arguing precisely that. The other says that it is lip service, that our issues, the ones that Gore was forced to contend with, will fade from the dialogue and from the agenda. No one, though, is in the mood to assess.

The atmosphere is festive. Emotion floods out in generous embraces. Rounds of drinks are bought and spilled. Shirts are untucked, unbuttoned, and in some cases fully removed. A colleague climbs onto a table. It collapses beneath his weight. There is laughter. People are tired of opinions and tears. They are reveling in camaraderie wrought by months of hope and hardship. They know that the man who brought them together is about to disappear and that when he does, their shared lives will also disappear. Many, myself included, stay out until six in the morning dancing, drinking, and carousing without moan, without sadness.

At noon, I wake up. I wake up loathing the light of day, knowing that with it comes no urgency of purpose. I long resented the urgency of purpose that so defines life on the campaign trail; I resented being always bombarded with responsibility; I resented having my thoughts and time swallowed by a single object. But it became routine. I grew accustomed to the pace. I developed a dependence. It will be difficult to forfeit this, to extricate myself from the perpetual high of movement and duty. I wake up loathing the light of day because the addiction that has sustained me is gone, because there is not much time left on the campaign and what remains is sure to be an extended wake of the most excruciating proportions, because the ogre of no job and no apartment snickers at me from the horizon.

The withdrawal speech is on March 9, two days after election night, in West Orange, New Jersey, at a hall near national head-quarters. It's a news conference, a media event. The general public is not in attendance. Reporters mill about, interviewing staff members. None of us is willing to work for Gore; this is their story. It does say something. Bradley inspired a strong loyalty, a loyalty that candidates don't always inspire, and Gore is not a likely replacement. To us, at best, Gore is a cowardly man, a man who tries to be all things to all voters. To us, at best, Gore is the stereotype of a politician.

Jay hangs black-and-white photographs of Bradley on a wall behind the podium. On a table at the opposite end of the room, there is a paltry spread of food. In between, there are chairs. The chairs fill, and I wait.

Bradley arrives with his wife, Ernestine. He begins promptly: "I've decided to withdraw from the Democratic race for president." He speaks with characteristic aplomb and straightforwardness.

I lean against a window. The glass feels cold. The reporters sit politely in rows, listening, attentive. I watch them. Their expressions are unfamiliar to me. I realize that I, unlike most members of the advance team, know few of them personally. There are faces to which I can't even attach names. I feel, for the first time, deeply curious about their lives.

A campaign is like an extended job interview, and our interview was conducted, in large part, by these people. When I decided to work for Bradley, I didn't understand this. I didn't understand the extent to which the media determine who runs and who wins. I didn't consider the extraordinary power they hold. Our press corps, composed of a relatively small group of men and women, passed to the public its evaluation through words, through chosen images, and on the basis of that there was a vote. It reported our perceived strengths, and we were the front-runner; our perceived weaknesses, and we are withdrawing.

This group of men and women traveled around the country with us as we fought for the presidency and radically altered our future, our evolution. I wish I had spent more time trying to understand them. I had ample opportunity. They stayed in our hotels and rode on our buses. They ate with us and drank with us. It was the advance staff's duty to anticipate their needs, to make sure that their bags got to their hotel rooms on time and that their risers were the right distance from the stage. We were repeatedly told that they like to be accommodated. We had little control over how well they were accommodated by our candidate, but we could make sure that we accommodated their desire for comfort and convenience.

The media were a physical presence in our lives. Yet I couldn't disengage from my emotions for long enough to look. I avoided them because I resented their articles and their news flashes, which I often thought were unfair and irresponsible. I resented the fact that they would report Gore's accusations without indicating whether or not Gore was telling the truth and then call it objective journalism. I resented them, so I never studied them. I was emotionally incapable of shuffling free of my distaste for long enough to acquaint myself with their personalities and motives, strategies and viewpoints.

Bradley's voice floats into my reflections. I turn toward him. He appears serene. He appears at ease. I am glad for him. I am glad too that the media will have no fatigue, no sour looks of defeat, to report.

I will also continue to work for a new politics and for the values I laid out in the campaign. What do I mean by creating a new politics in America? I mean a politics that's not polluted by money; a politics in which leaders speak from their core convictions and not from polls or focus groups; a politics that's about lifting people up, not tearing your opponent down; a politics that reflects the best of what is in us as Americans and not the worst; a politics that inspires us all to live up, or try to live up, to our potential as citizens and human beings . . .

The press conference ends with questions and then a warm round of applause. After the applause, Bradley gives each member of the press corps two gifts: a box of the lozenges he sucked audibly during events, and a key chain with a silver basketball shoe from Tiffany & Company. Then he is out, gone. I don't move. The room empties.

When the campaign began, the air was full of possibility. Pundits dropped to their knees. Pollsters were giddy. Bradley was the man poised to topple a sitting vice president. He was a paragon of virtue, a lofty vision of high ideals, the answer. Then he fell. I have tried to understand the forces behind that fall. I have tried to understand how events might have played themselves out differently.

I suppose his fall was caused in part by the loftiness, by the very virtue that we praised. Directly after my arrival in Iowa, Gore went on the attack when previously he had chosen to ignore us. People responded to Gore's aggressive new image, but Bradley didn't hit back. He said that it takes discipline to be positive. He said that negative campaigning is bad for America, bad for politics, and I loved him for it. The problem is that people thought him wimpy rather than brave. They likened him to meat being torn apart by wolves. The problem is that attacking, negativity, works. The lesson might be that good guys can't win, that there is no place in politics for high ideals, or it might be that there are no single meanings, no single identities, that compromise is a political necessity and not always a bad one.

Anyway, in retrospect, I have to concede, being all of one campaign wiser, that Bradley probably could have attacked Gore's policies and shortcomings, he probably could have pointed to his weaknesses and even to his lies, without being petty or unjust. He could have drawn the contrast between himself and his opponent more clearly. He also could have rebutted the attacks, but he wasn't willing. His lust for the presidency wasn't that strong.

Winning has a lot to do with appetite. Bradley never had the same appetite for power as Gore. That appetite was bred into Gore's personality. Theodore White once wrote: "The first and most essential quality of a Presidential candidate . . . is that . . . he should want [the job] more than all things, with a passion surpassing all emotion and probably even all principle." Gore had this. He wanted the job more than all things. Bradley, on the other hand, was wary. The sobering concerns of the presidency, the trappings of power, had lessened his ambition. He wasn't hungry for taste of the battle. I liked that. I thought that was healthy, but that didn't help us. And in the end, when Bradley finally tried returning the fire, it was too late. He appeared desperate, graceless. His heart wasn't in it.

The AFL-CIO's endorsement of Gore was another turning point. There were lots of turning points, but this sticks out in my mind, perhaps because it made real for me the idea of entrenched power. I saw the system at work. I saw it stretch out like a weed over a vast expanse. It reminded me of the New Jersey Meadowlands, where a hollow and self-perpetuating grass is all that exists, all that can be seen.

The endorsement came, as did Gore's attacks, soon after my arrival in Iowa, toward the beginning of October. Our campaign was taking off. Gore was struggling. At first, the unions were split. Many opposed making a decision so long before the national election. Ultimately, though, under heavy pressure from President Clinton, they folded, at least enough of them folded for the endorsement to go through. Clinton called J. J. Barry, president of the eight-hundred-thousand-member International Brotherhood of Electrical Workers. He set up a task force to look into the loss of manufacturing jobs. He moved to limit imports on low-priced steel, as part of an effort to placate the powerful United Steelworkers of America. And Gore had, in a flash, thirteen million men and women behind him, ready to print leaflets, to organize and mobilize.

Still, Bradley rose in the polls and stayed even in terms of fundraising. In fact, things went pretty well right up to the time of the heart incidents, which surfaced in December and then again in January. They were pretty insignificant medically, but the media squeezed every headline that they could out of them, and Bradley's image changed. People began perceiving him differently. He went from being a winning maverick, an antipolitician, to an object of pity and concern. He had to spend a great deal of time right before the Iowa caucuses convincing the American voters that he would be in no way inhibited as president. And the media grew more negative. They did not post pictures of what they saw on a daily basis, of enthusiastic crowds and a vigorous candidate; rather, they posted pictures of him lying in bed with his feet up, looking sick. For the media, it was a self-fulfilling prophecy. Bradley felt fine, the doctors said he was fine, but they set before the world pictures of him on what might be construed as his deathbed. Bradley was no longer the force behind the storm. He was tossed up into the storm like Dorothy and Toto. The sense of challenge disappeared. Our winner image was gone like Kansas.

The polls in Iowa reflected our changing fortunes. Yet we barreled ahead with the same Iowa-centered strategy. This appears to have been a mistake. It was too late to talk about skipping Iowa altogether, but it wasn't too late to change with changing fortunes. Devoting virtually the entire month of January to a state that seemed fated to spurn us was not sensible, though of course it is easy to say these things in hindsight. At any rate, no good came of it. In fact, staying in Iowa and losing was a deathblow. It gave our correspondents fodder for their stories of decline, and it undermined us in New Hampshire, a state that had long favored our candidacy.

If instead we had spent the month of January, even half the month of January, in New Hampshire, then we might have come away with a win, we might have dampened the impression that an Iowa loss was of such importance. But we waited to go to New Hampshire. We waited until McCain, another insurgent, had his chance to siphon away votes and media attention. We waited until the media had their chance to write "loser" all over us, and then we went to New Hampshire, with only a week left before the primary. Still, despite all of this, the results in New Hampshire were extremely close, but our crew of reporters didn't care to spin things sympathetically. They were already wrapped up in stories of our decline.

Bradley's relationship with them didn't help. Other politicians courted the media. They did their best not only to pamper them, to put them in the best hotel rooms, to cater to their desire for ease and comfort, but also to give them the access they covet. Bradley dismissed them. At events, he wanted to answer questions from the public, not the media. He didn't schmooze with them on the buses or planes, and when he felt their questions were ill timed or intrusive, he either refused to answer or was clipped and snappish. Again, I thought it was endemic to the characteristics we praised, to the fact that he cared more about substance than style, less about the con game, less about his celebrity, and more about the voter; but it wasn't good politics.

We made mistakes. Bradley was a flawed campaigner. The media were unfair. The stars weren't aligned. You could opine any and all of these things, but the fact is that even if the stars had been aligned, even if all the pieces had fallen into place, we probably still wouldn't have won. We were up against a sitting vice president with strong party backing. This is a huge advantage, nearly insurmountable, especially when the economy is experiencing its longest expansion in history.

A pain in my knee forces its way, like an alarm clock, into my reverie. The press corps and my colleagues have long since gone. The paltry spread of food that was on the table at the far end of the room is gone. The podium is gone. The room is quiet the way a stadium is quiet after the fans leave. I head toward the door. A stack of photographs lies in a pile on the floor. I stop and flip through them. They are campaign photos. Bradley tips his hat to the press corps and smiles ironically as he brushes by its cameras. Bradley, Bill Russell, and Cornel West stand together, laughing wide-open laughs. Bradley hugs Ernestine on a runway. Bradley has one fist embedded in an Everlast boxing bag and the other cocked to fire. Bradley descends from a stage into a sea of outreached hands. I leave the photographs in a stack on the floor and drive to headquarters.

I saw headquarters for the first time last September, the day I interviewed with the compliance department. I wore a light grayish green suit. I walked up from the bus stop trying to pronounce the word *constituents*, which had caused me to stumble earlier. I walked into the building without any idea of what I would find. Politics was foreign to me. I didn't know what caucuses were. I had never voted in a primary. I didn't really even understand why I wanted to work on a campaign or why I found Bradley to be such a compelling figure. I certainly didn't see any connection between Bradley and my father.

I park my car and turn off the ignition. Gabe knocks on my window. It startles me. He laughs. I smile. "Hey, we're heading to Chili's for lunch. Meet us there," he says.

"OK," I say without moving.

I grew up believing, as I suppose many children do, in dreams, in fairy tales. It was because of my father. People often think it necessary, once children reach a certain age, to rebuke their idealism. That wasn't my father. He wasn't the sort to say, "Ah yes, when one is young, one has castles in the air." He always had castles in the air. His favorite writer and theologian was G. K. Chesterton, who wrote: "The things I believed most then, the things I believe most now, are the things called fairy tales. They seem to me to be entirely reasonable things. They are not fantasies: compared with them other things are fantastic. Compared with them religion and rationalism are both abnormal . . . Fairyland is nothing but the sunny country of common sense." I grew up believing, because of my father, that dreams and ideals were something practical, something that could be maintained.

Then, just as I was facing life, just when I had met with things that might undermine those beliefs, he got cancer and later had a stroke. He was filled with fear when once he had seemed fearless. Maybe that fear had always been there, but I know that he himself was surprised to find it. He died believing in nothing. He died in a state of total despair, and I thought I lost all that he had given me.

Then there was Bradley, a man utterly different from my father, but a man who also believed in dreams and ideals. He was a practical man, who understood the limitations of government and politics yet maintained and expressed an idealism. This caught my attention. He was even, as it turned out, paternal, telling me not to go outside without a coat. He floated above my life for a while, and it felt good to have him there.

Oddly, though, it may be in failure that Bradley is most impressive to me, most, to put it plainly, useful to me. My father became horrifically ill and lost, though one could hardly blame him, his courage, his belief in fairy tales. Bradley failed but was unchanged by failure. I guess that you could call my father the thesis and Bradley the antithesis, which leaves me to synthesize.

What is certain is that Bradley restored something to me. He helped me to relearn, after ugly losses and countless confusions, the meaning of the word *hope*. My father used to say: "If a thing's worth doing, it is worth doing badly." It was a G. K. Chesterton line. I found it annoying. I didn't really understand it. I have, though, come to understand it. We built something, those of us on the campaign, and it crumbled, as most things do, but it was worth the fight, and it left me with, among other things, a certain political awareness without apathy and a sense that the world keeps rotating win or lose. I don't mean this to sound trite. I don't want it to seem as if I think there's some grand unifying theory of the world, because I don't, or at least I don't any longer.

I know that my father and Bradley have both been bound in my own mythology. My father died in the midst of things, and it was still possible for me, who was under his spell, to worship him, to believe that my whole life and desire for faith would have been solved if only he had never gotten sick. And with Bradley there is the temptation to say that if only he had succeeded, he would have set the world on the right path – and I do think that Bradley would have done wonderful things for America, but the wonder-working powers of single individuals are, I realize, limited.

My life intersected with politics. All lives, whether there is an awareness of it or not, intersect to some degree with politics, which of course is why voting is so important, which is why voting is just another way of exercising control over your own existence. Anyway, synthesizing my life and politics should be no different really from synthesizing my life and my father's death, my life and fairy tales. It involves finding a middle ground between the world of idealism and the world of more practical political realism. I once believed that it was one or the other. I had an unoriginally childish wish for a definitive answer. I wanted saviors and culprits, truths and falsehoods. This world will, however, always be tottering between doubt and belief, good and evil.

I want suddenly to lie down. I try to remember how long ago Gabe knocked on my window. It might have been five minutes. It might have been thirty. I decide that I can't possibly meet them for lunch at Chili's. I don't want to go into those offices, either. In fact, I want to lie down and be driven. I want to be lulled like a child toward comfort and sleep by the steady sensation of wheels moving over pavement.

I decide to go back to New York and to Flo. I have not spent time with her in weeks. I suppose relationships are just like anything else. I suppose that they are no place to look for absolutes. I suppose too that she already knew this, which is probably why she has been able through my absence and total preoccupation to remain patient and loving. The night is restful. She and I go to a movie.

The next day and then again on my last day, I return to national headquarters in West Orange, New Jersey. And I stand, a few hours before leaving finally and forever, in the corner of a supply closet, folding masses of soft, damaged banners and winding heaps of long, tangled sound cords. People bounce basketballs outside in the parking lot. In the next room, colleagues exchange addresses and sort through lingering receipts. I would rather wind cords. I work slowly. When I finish, I stand uneasily above the cords, reluctant to leave. I unwind a few already wound cords and wind them again into tighter, more even loops.

After a time, I look for the tall blond woman who is in charge of health insurance. She is sitting at a large, uncluttered desk. She anticipates my questions. I can maintain coverage for up to a year with low monthly payments. She calculates the cost. She provides the paperwork. She hands me a nicely organized and neatly labeled manila folder. I am overwhelmingly grateful to her, mostly because her voice is cold and unemotional. Her clean, plain facts float freely above regret. She nods and I leave.

The hall outside her office is hot. I think of the clean, plain facts, wishing that I could hover with them above her desk. Instead I stand stiffly, imagining myself as an inanimate object, as a lamp or a dividing wall. I am staring straight ahead at nothing in particular when Bradley walks past.

He looks oddly bare without his Secret Service protection, without his parade of staff and supporters. I notice his shoes, which look new. He offers a low, generous hello. I return his hello with something sadder, more defeated. Then, as I watch him disappear, fear saturates my limbs, my heart, and my neck. It is fear of the nothing that follows and fear of his absence. I call after him.

"Do you want to play basketball with me?" I ask.

My words clatter and sink. I look down and close my eyes, feeling embarrassed, praying that I wasn't heard. He pauses. I look up. His chin is lowered and he is smiling. Yes, he does want to play basketball with me.

Four men are on the court. They grin sheepishly at the tall hero.

"Joan" – he gestures toward me – "and I will accept any challengers." His voice fades in a laugh.

Two men step forward and offer Bradley a ball. A small crowd has already gathered. They are watching a former New York Knick, a former presidential hopeful. My shots soar and drop, magically. I think of Jack and the Beanstalk and of Cinderella. We win, and two more men step forward. The crowd has grown much larger. It would seem that the entire staff is watching, that the entire neighborhood is watching. There are cameras, there is music, and there is applause. It is real. We win again. We win swiftly and fondly. Our final opponents step forward. Our shots fall to increasing roars of pleasure. We win yet again.

A NOTE ON THE AUTHOR

Joan Sullivan lives in New York City and currently teaches American History at the Bronx School for Law, Government and Justice, a public high school in the South Bronx, where she also founded and coaches the girls' varsity basketball team. She spent two years working for the New York City Civilian Complaint Review Board, the city agency that investigates police misconduct. She is a 1995 graduate of Yale College, where she majored in American Studies. This is her first book.

A NOTE ON THE TYPE

The text of this book is set in Adobe Garamond. It is thought that Claude Garamond based his font on Bembo, cut in 1495 by Grancesco Griffo in collaboration with the Italian printer Aldus Manutius. Garamond types were first used in books printed in Paris around 1532. Many of the present-day versions of this type are based on the *Typi Academiae* of Jean Jannon cut in Sedan in 1615.

Claude Garamond was born in Paris in 1480. He learned how to cut type from his father and by the age of fifteen he was able to fashion steel punches the size of a pica with great precision. At the age of sixty he was commissioned by King Francis I to design a Greek alphabet, for this he was given the honourable title of royal type founder. He died in 1561.